Love Unconditionally

TO LOVE AND ACCEPT YOURSELF UNCONDITIONALLY

CANDACE GRANT

Candace Grant
Love Unconditionally

Published by BooxAi
ISBN: 978-965-578-031-4

Contents

To my children, Dalton, and Jade

Life may not always be what we want, but it will always provide the lessons we need.

Foreword

If you had to describe your life's goal in one sentence, what would it be? For me, it is simple:

To learn how to love and accept myself unconditionally.

It is easy to get lost in the chaos of our everyday living. Even when we are consciously searching for our purpose and our identity, we often look to others to fill the void, answer our questions, or assuage our loneliness and our happiness. But the only true answers come from within. When we allow others to determine our worth and diminish our authenticity, we literally give away our most sacred power. The power of Self-determination. Once we acknowledge this pattern, our universe begins to shift. We transition from living in the land of "conditions" (both self-imposed and imposed by others) to living and loving ourselves unconditionally.

My own journey to learning to *Love Unconditionally* took me on a bumpy road as I struggled to accept and love myself through loving someone with addictions, suicide attempts, mental illness, parenting, codependency, deaths, and forgiveness. My hope is that my life lessons will help you rediscover your voice, your identity, and the ability to love yourself unconditionally, just like I did. Once we recognize our biggest challenge is establishing proper boundaries, accepting a new love within ourselves (and others), we realize that our worth is non-negotiable... with anyone. Rediscovering your identity can be frightening as you navigate the "unbecoming" of everything you knew. My hope is that you get to live a truly happy life, always knowing YOU are enough for you.

About the Author

Candace Grant is a strategist coach. Her years of experience come from understanding that the body manifests pain and stress from daily life. Her mission is to teach you how to Love yourself worthy of everything you deserve through setting boundaries and manifesting your dreams. She is a mother, a daughter, a sister, a friend, a wife, an entrepreneur, and most importantly, an everyday woman like you. This is her true, often painful yet ultimately rewarding story of her challenges and her healing journey.

Love Unconditionally

"**Unconditional love**" **is the ability to love someone without limits, it is unchanging and unselfish. You want happiness for the other person regardless of the outcome or effect it has on your life.**" - Wikipedia

The truth is this: I did not learn how to love unconditionally until I was truly tested. Sure, we all claim to know how to do it. We all claim that we are doing it! And then we are pushed to the absolute limit and realize we have no clue what it really means to love unconditionally.

Think about *your* definition. How do *you* love without condition?

If you're like me, you probably switch back and forth from knowing how to *perceive* love to how you actually *do love* and accept others (and yourself) on your journey. Yes, the challenge is immense. Because even when we know what we should do or how we should react, we continue to take things personally and create unrealistic expectations that are unattainable. We completely forget that no one can ever be 100% the person we want them to be. Which is funny because we do not expect to be perfect ourselves, so how can we possibly expect someone else to achieve this lofty standard? Just think how difficult it is to change your own thoughts, habits, and patterns. How can we possibly believe it is our duty to change someone else?

The truth is we all change only when life tells us we must. When we are taught a lesson, we cannot ignore. When the pain of remaining as we are by far outweighs the fear of becoming something new. And through it all, we remain perfectly imperfect.

Let's be clear: unconditional love does not mean no restrictions and no boundaries. It does not mean loving no matter what. Unconditional love does not mean unconditional tolerance of negative, abusive, or destructive behavior. Unconditional love is more about accepting someone in their true authenticity. Allowing them the safety of being seen and heard even at their most vulnerable self.

But we struggle because we are conditioned to place boundaries and restrictions on ourselves. Therefore, just as was done to us as children, we feel a need to place boundaries and restrictions on those around us. I honestly used to think that unconditional love meant no restrictions or boundaries. But that definition no longer makes sense to me because it is impossible to facilitate. Whether we know it or not, we all superimpose our values, opinions, and ethics onto others. The trick is to set values for yourself whilst accepting the values of others, which are completely unrelated to yours. You always have a choice to agree or disagree.

It took me a long time to realize that my core values, created and defined by me over many years, are different from the core values of those around me. Look at it this way: we share our wisdom with our children, who in turn learn from other peers and mentors. We are all the sum of these many parts and of our own successes, failures, and experience. We create our boundaries based on the comfort of experience or the emotions we attach to them. Our boundaries continue evolving as we learn to integrate our experiences and emotions into our new perspectives. As we age our values, priorities and attitudes mature as we come to understand and empathize not only with our own life experience but with that of those around us.

Conditional love is, by its very definition – selfish. The conditions must be right for us (not the one we love), and those conditions become restrictions, rules or ultimatums that we expect *will* be followed. Even without acknowledging it, we demand that our loved ones fit into *our* box perfectly. Boundaries are something quite different. With boundaries we allow someone to be exactly who they are, and then we decide if their behavior is acceptable to us. If it is not, we then decide what guidelines we need to put into place to still accept that person as they are whilst taking control of our own life. Boundaries allow each person in the relationship an opportunity to both love the other and treat them with respect.

Unconditional love may be seen as love without limits, but it truly comes down to the understanding that the person you love has both positive and negative characteristics. As do you yourself. With unconditional love we strive to accept those negative attributes without judgement. However, do not confuse the tolerance of abuse of any kind with unconditional love. Abuse is not love, nor should it be normalized. If you choose to accept abuse by defining it as unconditional love, you will soon discover that you have stopped loving yourself.

It is important to see people for their strengths and not their weaknesses. This is one of those phrases, "easier said than done." Trust me, "I am trying." We blame others for how they are (and usually the way we are), not how we interpret the situation as it pertains to our feelings. That is what it is about, let us be honest, it is about OUR FEELINGS. It is easier to blame others for doing us wrong, making us feel bad or unimportant. It is easier to put the responsibility on others rather than see things as they truly are and take ownership of everything in our lives, all that we are, and all we have become. It is about knowing that someone did not follow your expectations, realizing "it is what it is" and moving on. People react based on their thoughts and feelings; their choices are made mainly because of who they are and not because of our role in their lives. Take yourself out of the scenario and chances are the outcome would be the same. Everyone's belief is different. That is what makes each person or situation unique. Most people do not stop and look at life this way. It took me awhile, but I am in a slow learning progression. "Life lessons will be repeated until learned."

Loving someone unconditional is possible when you learn to have acceptance for who you are and they are. You learn to see them and hear them for all they are, nothing more and nothing less. Sometimes we think we love someone unconditionally; we also realize that we did not really know what it meant as we tolerated their behavior thinking that it was love. We need to learn to love ourselves unconditionally first.

The whole goal in life is not about learning to love someone else unconditionally but learning to love and accept ourselves Unconditionally.

In my journey to loving myself unconditionally, I realized that the only way to get there was by accepting myself unconditionally first and foremost. Subconsciously I put conditions on love because I always put conditions of worthiness on myself. We are our own worst critics. I wanted to control all the people in my life as a sense of belonging or feeling significance. I told myself, "They needed me." Somehow, I never felt good enough. But everything I was feeling was rejection from the stories I kept repeating to myself.

In this journey, I realized so much about others through accepting myself. I could let go of who I thought I was supposed to be. I found a way to appreciate love and acceptance from the peaceful place of who I truly am. I found my higher self. I am enlightened by how much happiness and self-fulling joy and gratitude I have daily. I was able to forgive and heal myself and my relationships. I let go of not feeling enough for anybody to love myself, and always being enough for *me*. Through deeper shadow work, I've discovered I can allow others their journey, accept them wholeheartedly and love each of us unconditionally. One of the greatest things I learned along the way was that I could be generous and still set boundaries, a fundamental part of being able to love yourself.

After my journey and all my life experiences, my version of the definition is ***"Unconditional Love" is the ability to love and accept yourself and others without requiring a change of the person they are. A pure unlimited acceptance of love.*** Unconditional love is more about acceptance. You want happiness and other people to be happy, regardless of the part you play in their life. Love is not selfish, and you want the best for someone else. With true love we find true acceptance. When we unleash our own self judgement and ego, we release the control of others, allowing everyone to live life on their terms. This is the start of what loving unconditionally means and feels like. We may not always agree with other people, but we learn to have acceptance. We all want to love unconditionally, but few find that true love in someone else. We love our children or our animals this way. Most people only *think* they love this way, few do.

Unconditional Love starts with loving and accepting yourself first.

My Story

HAVE you ever wondered what happened in my life? How did I get here?

I fell in love with a wonderful person. We enjoyed life to the fullest, and then it felt like everything went to shit one day. How did I go from this amazing mom, full of energy and this great partner, to what felt like uncontrolled chaos? Eventually, I became unconscious in my daily life. I was going through the motions of trying to be everything for everyone yet losing myself deeper into an abyss.

I missed all the red flags I should have seen from the beginning that love blinded me from. Suddenly I realized the things everyone else already saw. My family had become dysfunctional! My partner's addiction had become the center of our life. I felt like the kids only talked to me when they needed me. The arguing escalated. Then I would convince myself to hold it together for one more day. I felt so drained every day, trying to be everything for everyone, yet feeling like no one was there for me. I felt torn between so many directions that I was soulfully exhausted at the end of each day. I did not need sleeping pills to sleep. I had no time to feel depressed or any emotions at all for that matter. It was all I could do to keep going. All I felt was, everyone relied on me, and they would never make it in this world without me. I am the glue holding everything together.

One day it happened. Slowly I regained consciousness and realized it was time to reclaim my life, figure out my values and set some boundaries. I did not have a clue where to start. I finally realized all the things I was trying to control were out of my control. All the people I was trying to help, I realized I was enabling them. People are happy with you when you enable them. I was a co-dependent, trying to live everyone else's life, trying to make them all happy. You will never make everyone happy. I gave up my values to meet the needs I thought I wanted (love and connection). Most of all, I lost my voice to speak up for what I required. I did not see how much of my life I had lost by not setting boundaries within my relationship or with my children. These ongoing issues dripped into other parts of my life and work. Now that my eyes were open, I had to figure a way out of these shadows. I was stuck with the person I did not like anymore, Me.

I started taking courses and realized I was the problem. (Wow, that was a revelation!) I was trying to control others, but I was enabling them instead of empowering them to make the right decisions. I was not allowing the process of their journey. I was blaming them for not listening or taking my advice, and this was pushing everyone away. I wanted everyone to rely on me, so I kept busy doing all the work. I needed them to need me, so I tried to become everything to everyone. This is one of my coping mechanisms brought forth from childhood. I did not understand how to keep the peace and everyone happy without losing myself. As some of my family and core values started to fade, I became resentful and regretful. I resented my partner for taking advantage of my generosity and for allowing me to carry the responsibility of raising our four kids. I resented him for always having more fun than I could because I was the "responsible one." I resented him for his addictions and the fact he allowed his alcohol to take over his life and monopolize our time. It was his mistress. I regretted losing the connection with my children while I was so wrapped up in my partner's needs and his addictions. I was losing myself more each day by staying in a relationship in which I knew I was no longer happy. Yet, I wasn't ready to leave.

As I broke through my barriers and started identifying my values, I realized I had no boundaries, nor did I understand them. I expected that others should just follow my rules. I realized I had enabled everyone in my life, and they let me, which made me resentful. I started to shift my life by understanding the only reactions, feelings, and actions I could control were my own. Most times, all the disappointments I had were because I allowed my ego to get the best of me. I expected more from a situation or person that I had no control over. I complained about the situation but did nothing to change it. My life was never fulfilled as I was only focused on keeping the peace and everyone else happy, which never worked, nor was it the solution.

As I started to shift from my enabling patterns to setting boundaries, I started to allow others to make their own decisions with empowerment and encouragement. This permits natural consequences to happen. My life started to become happier. I stopped controlling others' actions and started focusing on rebuilding my life. Self–care became important, and all my relationships started to shift. Most importantly, I gained unconditional love for myself. I became my own best friend again. I was more confident in all my decisions and choices. When you start setting boundaries, you weed out people in your life that are there for the wrong reasons. Setting boundaries gave me a new respect for myself, plus I regained my voice to protect my values. I found my authentic self through practicing boundaries. I have a better relationship with my kids because I allow them to make their decisions with trust. Boundaries are never about the other person; it is about you and the consequences you are willing to tolerate. A sense of freedom happens when you stop enabling or focusing on other people's happiness. After all, that is a lot of power to have over someone else's life. My life became more passionate and fulfilled after I learned the difference between enabling and empowering. I learned through understanding my core values and boundaries that all of it is a part of learning how to accept and love myself.

Throughout my life, I have learned so many lessons and strategies for learning acceptance. I may have never learned, not having gone through this challenging relationship. I look at it as a gift. It was my greatest lesson. It taught me to look beyond the people in front of me, for there is always a deeper story behind it. Everyone hurts or heals from trauma differently. Everyone has a story that will break your heart. I have learned acceptance of myself. This helps me to accept others exactly as they are without trying to control them, change them or make them fit into my box or who I think they should be by my expectations. By loving myself unconditionally, I can speak my truth from my heart without fear or self judgement. I understand my core values. I am not afraid to live guilt-free from my decisions (my prerequisite of doing no harm to others). My definition of living guilt-free is following your heart and giving from a place of love, and not fear-based.

I had many trials and tribulations in learning to love myself and the ability to empathize and understand with acceptance of the challenges in my life. Sometimes amid chaos and daily life, we do not see the struggles everyone has as we become so focused on our own life and meeting our own needs. We overlook the meaning of the lessons and the gifts that everyone in our life brings to us. Everyone you meet will teach you something about yourself if you are willing to learn and grow from the experience.

Family

I HAVE RAISED two children of my own, plus my two stepchildren for 11 years. For each of them I have learned more about myself than I did growing up. We were put together to learn from one another. Experience has taught me, that we must first look inward and take self-inventory of the criticisms we give others, the boundaries we overlook, our enabling patterns, the controlling issues, and our judgement, opinions, and the advice we give. This is a constant practice of taking a pause and asking yourself ... what is my intention? How may this be perceived? A lot of times we have good intentions, but bad delivery or bad timing. We may be able to set boundaries of what we tolerate yet still not recognize someone else's boundaries. We may have intentions of helping, yet it may come across as controlling or enabling. We may criticize and think it is helpful to point out the mistakes of others, but it may be upsetting to them. We may judge or give our opinion based on the part of a situation as we attach our own emotions or behaviors. When questioned, we become defensive in survival to protect our own ego. We give advice sometimes before we ask permission to give it. This is a constant battle with mastering your ego. Although we may be knowledgeable about what to do and can see it in others, sometimes we need to stop and be more mindful of ourselves.

We all have our own journeys to take, at different time periods and separate paths. We must remind ourselves to let others find their way. We have the best of intentions, especially when it comes to the people we love the most. We must remember we were young once and on our own path of making mistakes and learning right from wrong. We need to trust the process in their journey and accept that we sometimes need to take a backseat with our thoughts. We need to ask permission to share and have others hold space or permission to give advice. Being mindful is asking: "do you want my opinion, my advice, or just need to vent?" We need to learn that while sharing our boundaries, we need to respect the boundaries of those around us. You cannot fix a communication issue if no one is communicating!

In raising children, we learn that we are also finding new ways to accept ourselves, our imperfections, our weaknesses, and our strengths. We bring so much to the table of life that we do not understand the past hurt and trauma from our own upbringing that we subconsciously pass on to our children causing generational trauma. We want them to be more or have more than we may have had. Yet, at the same time, we do not see the damage we may be contributing by creating a life they do not know how to feel accepted in. They feel they are never good enough and have to strive to live up to everyone's expectations to feel loved. We need to let go of our own belief about how our children should be and just love them for who they are. This is unconditional love of our children. This is acceptance of ourselves and our past trauma by having the ability to surrender to it and move on.

When a blended family comes together, things shift in the family dynamic. Two people come together from different family values, experiences, and upbringings. Stress has a way of making life more difficult, as everyone can sometimes be pulled in many different directions. You may have a general sense of the same values, but as the family unit shifts, the branches of the values start too as well. We start to conform to someone else's belief system rather than our own. This sometimes is from expectations of outcomes or the lack of boundaries. We tend to enmesh with our spouse or our children, and everyone else's activities become more prevalent and important than our own. We simply lose our own life trying to micromanage everyone else's happiness. Eventually, as moms, we start to go into an automatic survival mode and coping mechanisms. We lose sight of our own direction and our own self-care. Families either become more definitive together or eventually, the matrix unit breaks down over time. Lack of communication, understanding, boundaries, external forces, and internal thoughts all play a part in this breakdown. All that is left is the memories of the most amazing times with the moments that everyone has a unique perspective of the same situation, "the tough times." Perspectives are like icebergs, everyone sees the top part that is visual. Still, each person has a distinct perspective which depends on their viewpoint, beliefs, expectations, and the emotion they give it. Therefore, we remember events or situations differently with the same scenario. We all give it a different emotion, which sometimes can feel like trauma.

In blended families, everyone feels left out from time to time. They do not feel their needs are being met, and everyone's needs are different yet are all the same. We all want trust, appreciation, significance, admiration, respect, certainty, growth, and most of all, unconditional love. We want someone to love us no matter the moment, no matter our mood, our flaws, or our strengths.... just love us the way we are. We will not always agree with everyone in our life, but we do our best to teach them how to handle the situation presented. With our children we try to teach them not to take things or people so personally. This is a valuable lesson for any age. People will try to hurt you and break you in life. Those moments are about them, not us. Even as adults we must learn this lesson. It is hard when others do not take feelings into consideration. Always be kind with words as they cannot be returned once they are spoken. Verbal abuse is never easy to deal with, especially from a child's point of view. Are you teaching them to neglect all they heard, or is it ok to speak to others like they are your punching bag? From a mother's point of view, it is straddled with conflict, as we like to think we do not believe people are truly trying to hurt one another. Instead, people are just clouded with frustration and anger and do not communicate or think before speaking. As parents, we are trying to teach all the lessons at once, and it seems challenging. Yes, it is impossible as life does not happen all at once, and people learn at contrasting times. Kindness is everything, but when someone is unkind, you must know that your own reaction is what matters most. Stand up for yourself, and do not let the words of others make you believe any less of yourself.

Most people would choose not to raise stepchildren if they had the chance to do it over. You try to love them and treat them equally, but it is just not the same. In the end, you have sacrificed many things to have them make you an option in their life. Your own children have also sacrificed their time and years of their needs being met. Some blended families get along, are fully committed, and have made it work long-term. It is all about being aligned with your goals and values.

To anyone that chooses to raise other people's children, have patience. Know your family values, goals, and communication. Work together and find the balance. Resistance from children is normal, it can be frustrating and challenging. Remind them who the parent is and stay on the same page as your parenting partner.

Parenting

We love our children unconditionally; we see their good qualities, and we accept their flaws. We are all hardwired for struggle, and sometimes our good intentions fall short. I love my children very much; they mean everything to me. Regardless of the issues we may have with our children. We never stop loving them. We go through periods where we do not like them very much because they do not conform to "our picture of them" set by our standards and our beliefs. What about their standards and their beliefs? At what age do they truly get to choose who they want to be as a person? Our role as a parent or a caregiver is to give them guidance to lead them in the direction of health and happiness. We need to remember that their choice of happiness may be different than ours. Love and support are always important, regardless of our opinion.

Parenting has changed and evolved over the years. We tend to tell our children that life is not about them, and this can be one of those conflicting statements. We want to teach them that life is all about me! It is My life, and I get to choose to live it the way I want. When everyone understands respect for others, taking responsibility for our actions, owning the reactions and consequences made by our decisions and accepting that you do not harm yourself or others. Unfortunately, the pendulum has swung so far, the other way with ME first that it has become a generation of many entitled children and adults. We treat others the way we want to be treated, but if others do not follow that same rule, we still treat them with respect but learn to walk away. Yet, we also want them to be strong enough to feel the courage to stand up and not allow someone to disrespect them or their feelings. We should also treat people how they want to be treated because everyone has different values and standards.

Children feel emotions and pain on vastly diverse levels than we do. Parenting is the toughest job there is and very contradictory. We cannot instruct our children about the world if we constantly try to save them from it. We want our children to be obedient and do what they are told when they are told. We want them to react to our expectations and behave in a manner suitable to our needs yet be strong enough to stand up for what they believe in. It is not about being a follower or being a leader but about following your own path and passion. Despite how we try to teach them, we want them to know what acceptable behavior is and what is not. We try to teach them to do as I say, not as I do. This comes from experience, age and because, as adults, we are still learning. Yet, we also what them to think for themselves and be themselves, yet what we really mean Is, if I approve. We are constantly trying to make them people pleasers by them seeking our approval, yet we want them to be proud of themselves. As parents, we cannot have it both ways. So, do you want an obedient people pleaser child who can only think when and is told and how to think? Or do you want a strong-willed person that stands strongly for what he believes to be true, despite what others think they should behave and do? Everyone is on their own journey, and the child takes in the qualities he needs to make him a stronger adult. I have a son who has presented many challenges to me on several occasions. I honestly think that of everyone I know, he has taught me more about life than anyone else. Always be who you are.

We put a lot of stress on our children these days, taking them from childhood to adulthood with a lot of responsibility and sometimes less understanding. Life has been altered with more things to do, more money to spend, and family time has changed. Families do not sit around the dinner table or have time together the same way we used to. Views of family time have changed. Growing up, it did not matter what we did as a family, it was family time. These days social media consume the attention of everyone in the family, and everyone lacks communication. Parents have a different view of the world than kids, and the generation gap of socialism has changed. Kids still like being with friends, but time usually includes a cell phone. It takes away from the one-to-one communication of just being present with the people that surround you and truly listening and enjoying their company.

Children still learn by examples. As the adults in their life, we are their examples. If you want to teach them, be the teacher they respect. Alter your teaching to them, not them to your teaching. Listen to learn, so they will learn to listen. Base your teaching on their needs, not your teaching needs or lack of understanding. We all learn differently, so why do we expect our children to be different? Why do we expect them to just get the lesson? Chances are we didn't the first time or second. We just hope that our children are smarter than us, just like our parents did. We are not our children's only teachers. Life has many teachers: school, society, peers, social media, and internet, to name a few. Some have good intentions, and some are difficult to see the true spirit and meaning. Everything they learn contributes to the person they will become someday. We all play a part in the future of our children. So be careful what you teach as it is not always interpreted the way we teach. As adults, we are our child's first role models, and they learn from our behavior. We do not get a choice; you are automatically a role model to your children (and their friends). The perspective you want them to learn is up to you. They will copy your words and your actions. We teach people what is acceptable to us by the behavior we allow. We need to communicate and listen better if we do not like how someone treats us. If you allow someone to treat you in a sense that is not acceptable, it builds resentment and hurt. Everyone hurts someone else without realizing it. However, it is about your integrity that follows. It is how you turn it around, apologize, change behavior, and take ownership. In teaching our children forgiveness, we must allow them to feel angry and work past it. We must validate their emotions with acceptance and understanding. I still struggle with this; it is a work in progress. This is hard for adults, just the same, especially if no one allows you to feel your own emotions. One of my favorite sayings is "***holding on to anger and resentment is like drinking poison and waiting for someone else to die.***"... ***Buddha***. If you are holding onto grudges from the past, you are the only one hurting in the relationship. Chances are, the other person is not allowing it to control them the same way. Let it go. The earlier we learn this in life, the happier life becomes. We are only restricted by our emotions. Sometimes holding a grudge or resentment is more about the emotion we attached to the experience and not the experience itself.

In creating boundaries in your emotional life, you must believe that *"when there is a choice between being right and kind, choose to be kind every time"*. Most people would rather be right to prove their point. It is a way for us to create significance in our mind. Most adults think that just being an adult makes them right but forget that not every child will conform to their thought process. Just because I am an adult and have more life experience with most things... does not mean I am the perfect human being or the perfect adult. Just because people read or are taught different beliefs does not mean they are right either. Life changes, and people are taught different perspectives of everything based on their teacher (or social media). Kids do not come with manuals and handbooks, so we parents do our best to love them unconditionally. Some parents do not know how to let go of the conditions of love. For kids and adults, always be willing to listen with the intent to learn from another perspective. Growing is learning. Our job as a parent is to pick up our kids when they fall, and be there as support and mentor. Never be judgmental. Acceptance of their choices. Cherish the moments, good and bad. Teach them all you can, and they will take what they feel is necessary for their life. Most times in life, we only use what is important now, and the rest is storage.

Children

As children grow older, they tend to push us away for a while. It is natural as we have pushed them away sometimes as little kids. We forget that just as we need adult time, they need friend time. Children tend to go through a phase that their other friend's parents are cooler. Although this sometimes hurts or frustrates us, we need to take a step back and remember not to take it personally. Our children will always come back to us if we are a good parent. I consider myself a good parent with many learning curves. I allow my children to follow their dreams but make suggestions when needed. Even if they do not listen at the time, I know it is in their head. I allow them time to grow and be with their friends. I love and cherish our time together. I try to teach them responsibility, lessons, never giving up and try to see the best in people. You cannot control anyone, only yourself. My children have the capability of being self-reliant and self-assured. I am immensely proud of my children every day.

Children feel that when their parents give them "unwanted" help or suggestions that they are not ready to accept or hear, this is the way of wanting to create perfection. Parents do not expect perfection from their children at all. We are doing the best we can to plant a seed and help it grow. To protect them from the same mistakes we made and learned from many years later. We all want to be perceived as unflawed and perfect. Yet no one is, we are all hard-wired for struggle. We only want to see our kids do their best; it is not the requirement of perfection they perceive. When our children feel the need to be perfect, they are afraid of their own vulnerability. They are afraid of the ability to show up and be seen in any emotional state they are in. I learned that I lacked validation of my children's thoughts, opinions, and feelings. I tried to be more empathetic in my daughter's life than in my son's, but I also started to regain consciousness of my parenting values in that period. It was time to trade in my superhero cape and get back to my beliefs and understanding! This was going to take some time.

Sometimes our children do not feel validated by the emotions they express. They feel they were not good enough or that they were not # 1 because we do not always agree with them or their choice. As parents, we do not always see from their perspective but from the whole picture. We interpret the situation based on perceived consequences or our experience. Everyone wants to learn as they go along. There are no right answers, as journeys are created around the individual. It is about timing and experience. As parents, we need to take a backseat unless their choices create harm to themselves or others. Our goal is to teach them not to live life holding on to grudges and creating bitterness. Learn to accept themselves and other people. We all have challenges in our own journey that we are meant to learn on our own time.

When our children were young, so many times they would fall, and we encouraged them to get back up. We did not laugh at their mistakes. We did not make fun of them. They have feelings like adults; an adult should not take away a child's right to feel. We tend to forget that their reactions to situations are relevant to their age, but most times, we expect them to react our way. Otherwise, it may not be good enough. We need to learn to let the child be, at the moment, with his feelings.

Our role as a parent is to love our children unconditionally. To teach our children that no matter what, we as parents are there to listen, support, and trust them to make the best decisions for them. Instead of telling them about the rules all the time, we need to ask their opinions and let them decide the outcomes. This is how we build trust, communication, and problem-solving skills for the future. They are ready to start their own journey in life and live life on their terms. As parents, we must learn to figure out our roles in our children's lives. We need to learn to ask permission to give advice and allow them to learn from their own experiences.

We forget there is a generation gap in life. What we grew up with and what was acceptable back then is unacceptable now. There is such a unique way of looking at life, from our grandparents, our parents to us, and now our children. We have already lived through four generations of change. I forget the struggle from the change of perspective from a child's point of view to an adult's perspective. I think we often fail as adults or parents to consider the feelings of a child or teenager. We know what we mean, but it is taken out of context or too literal by them. This is usually my bad timing, improper delivery, tone diversity, or overall miscommunication of comprehension. Their feelings get hurt, and we get frustrated as miscommunication is so common today. The lack of voice tone, misinterpretations, and lack of what we learned as respect. A way of life we learned is now being judged or questioned for its inappropriate teachings, racism, bullying, or discipline strategies. Everything is misjudged or out of context. Children are taught to look at and receive the world differently than we were taught. It becomes a fine line when you give children just as many rights and powers as adults. Children will tend to over judge a situation as unfavorable if it is against them rather than for their cause. We, as parents, are not always right. However, we still make the rules in our house, just as there are rules everywhere to be followed and respected even if not agreed upon by everyone. Situations of circumstance have improved a long way with more understanding, acceptance, and diversity with this generation. We still have a lot to learn from one another.

Both my children and my stepchildren have proven to walk their own paths, have their own beliefs, and follow their passions in their life. They are not followers or leaders. They are strong enough to stand on their own and able to challenge the issues they believe in. They are still learning in life, as we all are. They have taught me more about myself in the past few years about strength and love. They have challenged me in many ways with great lessons about life and perspective; in the end, we are all stronger.

All children are envious of one another. It does not matter if they are blood-related or just share common families. Let's be honest... nothing in life is ever equal or fair. As much as we try, life changes and demands change. Kids have different interests, which presents us with alternative needs and cost factors. We teach our kids to be thankful for all they have no matter what because things always work themselves out. It should never be about more or what someone else has. We, as parents, do the best we can. We are always wanting to give more, just as our parents did. However, more doesn't equal happiness, and having more may lead to the desire to have even more feelings of entitlement instead of the gratitude that was intended. Teaching your child to be a good and respectable person is a necessity. Sports and lessons are activities that teach children; self-confidence, respect for something, perseverance, leadership, team-work, dedication, and many other traits which are important for growth and individually.

We want an effortless way of life, yet we seem to add more to make it complicated. Any relationship can have its challenges. Parenting and relationships are about adaptability. As parents and partners, we must adapt many times throughout our life. I never looked at myself as a people pleaser until I was put in the middle of two people I love. How do you take sides when you can see both sides? How do you choose who is right and who is wrong? Why can't everyone just get along? Let me tell you. It is not easy to decide what is right for you if you allow everyone to demand all your attention. I learned that I have enough love for everyone in my life, and I do not need to choose nor make others choose. However, with a lack of boundaries, nobody wins. We are taught to put our spouse first and stand united to teach children values. Recently, society has shifted to put the needs of the children first, which can create a shift in the hierarchy system and an unbalanced harmony. Overall, we need to be sure about our own position and create goals with the needs of everyone in consideration. Otherwise, it becomes a situation of us against them in a system of failure.

As the years go by, our children change as they grow and mature. We realize as parents that despite the frustration, anger, constant battle of control, and micromanaging that they figure things out. We take our experiences and our knowledge and then add them to an open mind full of wonder and curiosity (with a little spice of ego from both sides), and we can get through it together. Learn to be open when listening to your children. Their perspectives are far greater than we usually give them credit for. They are not just learning from us but also all the other adults around them. They take a piece of everyone, and it contributes to their own person on their own journey. As my therapist taught me, "Listen to understand, not to respond. A great lesson for any relationship. My daughter is full of compassion and empathy, and my son is full of strength and passion. Yet, when I look again... I see the same is true for both, just in diverse ways. Sometimes as parents, we think about how amazing it is to have children of the same two parents be so different yet similar. We may see them as having different strengths. Certain areas of strength are more predominant at distinct stages of their life. Somedays, we realize they are not so different. You must be willing to see the whole picture. Although we try to raise our children with the same basic principles of life, the same ethics, and boundaries, life changes them with unique experiences as they both perceive a situation differently. Trauma is about the emotions we give to an experience or event. That is why some can let go, and some hold the experience for the rest of their life. We all obtain something different as we are supposed to from the same experience; that is why it is your *personal journey*. We learn our children do not respond and grow or learn the same way. Circumstances change lives. No one has every strength or attributes all the time. Life is about balance.

In taking a closer look at both my children, both resemble a part of myself, the good, the bad, and the imperfect. We need to step back in life and look at ourselves and our children. We expect them to be perfect in an imperfect world. We expect them to learn from our mistakes and wisdom. We expect them to behave as we feel is acceptable to us. We expect too much! Just as I have learned my lessons and grown with my life experiences, they will also. I trust they will both succeed in life, happiness, and love. My children are everything to me.

MY SON

My son, Dalton, has a passion and adventurous spirit. The love and exploration of the world. He loves to learn and has a thirst for knowledge. He has strength and determination and is extremely resourceful. I know I will never have to worry about him in life, but as his mom, I will always have my worries. I trust him to make the right decisions or at least learn from them. He is not a follower or a people pleaser. I have learned that he is a leader. He lives life on his own terms. Fear does not stop him. He decides and goes all in. He sets a goal and sees it through. Dalton has a thirst for knowledge and a drive to always be learning. At an early age he taught himself to play chess and various musical instruments. He is always taking chances on a new business venture. He is willing to try something new and does not usually back down when faced with adversity or a challenge. He will be successful in his life no matter the road he takes.

Reflecting from my perspective, my son portrayed a lack of empathy at times, but his values and beliefs were changing as he matured and saw the world from a different point of view. He will learn more empathy in time, with maturity and understanding. Part of his childhood coping mechanism of self-preservation was to not allow himself to feel or understand that someone has a unique perspective from how he feels or understands. He is very black or white with less grey in-between. He does not tell people what they want to hear as he does not want to seem fake but does not realize the hurt it has caused. He has had emotional hurt and does not realize that even when people hurt you, it is about them and their issues. It is not about you. The ego takes on that perspective many times until you can learn otherwise. This lesson took me 47 years to learn. Overall, people that hurt will hurt people. Sometimes all we see is our point without cause and effect. We do not realize that our actions can cause a reaction. Blaming others is part of not taking accountability for yourself. It is easier to blame others for our hurt and emotional upset, but it takes maturity to realize it is our expectations of others that are the real hurt and emotion. Sometimes his lack of listening and lack of communication skills are seen as disrespect and immaturity. However, with his belief system, you must earn his respect first before it is freely given, especially if you have already caused him pain. He has a strong belief in how he and others should be treated. I admire this quality in him. However, he still needs to learn that everyone is entitled to their own opinion, and it does not make anything less right or wrong. Judgment is in the eye of the person judging. Usually, judging others is because we have disowned that part of ourselves yet do not realize it. This takes many years to explore and understand. Do not waste your heart and soul on other opinions. Yet, always listen with the intent to learn, as others have a lot to teach us. In other words, take what you can and garbage the rest. Do not let the unimportant things of life overrule your life.

I do not always agree with my son, but I do love him and respect him. I get frustrated that he pushes my limits and beliefs to a varying degree, but that is what he is in my life to do. I have also come to realize he is finding his way in life. His journey in life is different than mine. I try to pick my battles better now that I understand his personality type. We are very opposite, or too much the same sometimes. Therefore, I would rather walk away from a debate that will result in disagreement. I choose not to have a conversation or confrontation. It is about having a relationship versus who is right. I am proud that he stands up for what he believes, but it frustrates me when he is unwilling to listen to others. As this is the perspective I see when I am in his presence. I am sure he will learn this in time with growth and maturity. We take different sides of the fence as he learns that sometimes how we want or expect life to be, unfortunately, just is not the way life is sometimes. I have learned the hard way that it is heartbreaking when we put expectations on others the way we want them to behave or act. He will also learn through experience and time. Our expectations of others are all about the US and the way we want the world and others around us to be. It is a hard truth when we realize that someone is like us and the issues that bother us are the ones we taught them or are because we are the same and just do not realize it. We recognize it more when someone else does it. I am sure his strong-willed mind may be a characteristic that goes with determination and a strong belief in his views and himself. He will learn in time the portrayal of confidence versus cockiness. Experiences in life will open minds, so you realize there is more gray area than anyone knew. That is where I am at.

There are many things I need to get real with when I look back at my parenting with my son. I did not recognize him for his sensitive emotions. I did not know how to allow him to just feel and be vulnerable. I did not recognize when I needed to just validate him and his feelings. I realize this now and understand that all my short-comings contributed to his personality now. Just as I was learning to guide him, he could not count on me or feel safe with the emotions he shared. I was scared and in survival mode. My mind was so wrapped around my own daily coping mechanisms that I did not stop and acknowledge the son that needed me the most. I was in my ego self. It was not about meeting his needs; it was about the day-to-day life of 4 kids, a home, a self-employed job, and a relationship that had many difficulties. This was my survival mode. For years I had become an unconscious parent. There are so many times I wish I could go back and hug him a little tighter and just validate his emotions.

My son has been able to set his boundaries of his worth and respect early in life. This is something I admire in him. It gives him strength and understanding that he is confident and needs to be appreciated. He will not tolerate any behavior that makes him feel inferior. These were lessons of emotions he learned in childhood. Never hustle for your worthiness. It is not up to anyone else to decide your worth. You are responsible for your own happiness and life.

Sometimes it is hard to let our children pave their future when trying to teach them what we think is a better way to do things. My son wants to step up and build a business, and this does not surprise me at all. He has always been a business-minded child. I commend him for his challenging work and enthusiasm. As a parent, I suggested never giving up a guaranteed income while starting a business venture. We need to have money to make money and find a balance between the two. New business is 100% effort and timing, with the mindset being 80% and the skills being 20%. It is about setting a goal, setting allotted time, and focusing on tasks, all while following passion and determination for success. We all need to find a balance in our life, as life does not stop for one task. We need to learn to prioritize and juggle many things going on. My son has what it takes for any business venture he chooses. He has that one quality most people lack, determination. He knows what he wants and goes for it. He thinks if people are against him (even if they are not), it drives him harder and further. Sometimes teenagers do not realize that asking questions and offering advice or suggestions does not mean parents or anyone is against them. We are just looking into the bigger picture. Teaching them that business is about passion and purpose. Finding your niche through services or products you offer and not just about money. These thoughts or ideas stem from experience and growth. From his standpoint, he felt a lack of trust and belief. In the end, we both want greatness, success, and happiness for him. I am proud that he is willing to take risks and chances, but he is cautious and self-taught while seeking advice from those he values the opinions of about his endeavors, "more than I will truly realize."

Dalton feels that I never took his side, some issues I never knew about or did not have the same perspective as he did. There were moments I went into freeze mode as it triggered my past of feeling helpless. I did not know whether the situation with the alcoholic would make it better or worse with confrontation. I stepped back as I watched the next step. I went to the same survival mode as I knew as a child, watching people drink and fight and feeling helpless. I did not always protect him at the moment. I realize that now. There is always more than what they see. I always had his back, even if he did not know or see it. Eventually, when children do not trust their parents, they stop coming to them. They do not ask their advice and lose that bond. These are the things that build the personality and character of our children. Our lack of conscious parenting. Children do not see the moments we struggle, knowing we could have made different choices or the times that we put their needs before our own. The times we defended them when they were not around with all we have in our hearts. Or the times we cried to ourselves, knowing we hurt so bad for the missed opportunities we had, but we were so "busy" with things we thought were important at the time that really was not. Reflection of ourselves and our learning curve is great, but it does not change the past. It allows us to understand why our boys grow into men that struggle. We want our boys to be strong, yet do not teach them to be vulnerable. We prevent them from emotions or do not validate them. We have an expectation of how they should behave, react, and feel. We want them to communicate yet do not really listen and communicate properly. We want them to have the ability to apologize, yet we never teach them how to give a proper apology. Most of these things we do not teach because we've missed opportunities to learn them ourselves. We expect boys to grow up and be men, to just know how to be loving, nurturing, protective and strong. We want them to be much more than we usually teach them as parents because we lacked it in our upbringing. Therefore, men struggle with communication and emotions by trying to be it all when never having learned. If I could go back in time, I would have done so many things differently, but I was learning to parent, just as he was learning to be a child.

My unconditional love for my son, Dalton, is about accepting that we may not agree with our opinions or perspectives. I understand his need for significance and certainty between our boundaries. I acknowledge the issues I may not have had in the past. Together we will build a better foundation. I love him for the young man he has become and value his resourcefulness for his future. I have been able to watch my son grow, take responsibility and ownership, and realize that someone always knows more than you. His job positions have taught him more compassion and empathy, plus many life skills of maturity. I am extremely proud of the person he has matured into. He has had many hard lessons along the way that have shaped him into the person he is today. Through his upbringing, he learned that the greatest gift a parent can teach is independence and the ability to care for yourself. Some kids never learn this as their parents enabled them. My son's independence will make him a better man, which is important for his everyday life.

The hardest pill I had to swallow recently was a conversation we had when he told me that if I were not his mom, we would not be friends. At first, it was like a knife stabbing me in my heart and I wanted to break into tears. I have sacrificed and craved his love and forgiveness for all the years. I sat with my emotions for the day and realized he was right. We are quite different in our personalities and views. His view was he did not know "who I was." He did not know my hobbies, my interests, and my goals. I did not share with him my life other than as his mom. He didn't realize my cooking background as I cooked simply, pleasing six different people. He figured that the person I was with was the only reason I took on certain hobbies or interests. My biggest interest is learning new things. As adults, we change and adapt to our relationships. At the end of the day, he said all he knew about me was that I loved him. To me, that is the most important memory he can have. I have done my job.

Overall, my son and I have a good relationship now. We can talk but still have our issues we work through. I know more about his needs and what he needs from me as a parent. I am learning my role in his life. I am sure this will shift many times as we learn together and start to break down the emotions of the past and move forward in building a new and better relationship. I cannot take away his pain from the past, but hopefully, I can build trust for our future. I hope when he remembers the past, he will remember not only the bad parts of his childhood but also all the good. All the time I was there for him, everything I did for him, and not just the years I struggled to maintain the "happy household." Our children will always have a different perspective of their childhood than we have as parents.

My son has matured into a fine young man, and I am proud of his journey. He knows his worth in life. He is willing to try any job to pay his bills but continues chasing his dreams and achieving his goals. He sets a high standard for himself. We have reached a place where I am happy to say we are friends as well as mother and son. Parenting is all about trials and errors, and I have made a lot. But one thing I could always count on was my son teaching me the right way that he needed me to parent him. What worked for him was to build our foundation of trust, love and understanding. We now have an amazing bond. I do not see him very often, but I appreciate our quality time together. Each child teaches you about who you are as a parent, as their teacher, as their supporter and more about yourself.

MY DAUGHTER

My daughter, Jade, has a beautiful heart and is willing to help anyone. She has the strength of a leader, the compassion of an empath, and the heart of a warrior. She knows her beliefs and is never afraid to stick up for what she believes. I have learned to value her opinions and view. When I struggled with the perspective from adult to child, I relied on her to set me straight. She sees life from different angles, usually without a biased conclusion. Unfortunately, this has also created a strain on our relationship. She had felt put in the middle a few times when she was still only a child and learning herself. The love she puts into a situation is usually in the form of believing in her brother. (My biggest understanding challenge at one point). She could explain things from a unique perspective. In fact, both my children have this quality (I think it is a generational thing). I used to believe in treating others the way you want to be treated, yet I found it difficult to stand up for other people's feelings through validation (Fear of making a situation worse from my teenage years). That is where she comes in. She made me realize that some things are not as they appear to be. Looking at situations harder is some-times necessary. This was when I lacked the perspective of the bigger picture. Instead, I only saw the parts I felt were important at that moment of time. She is my guiding angel and has helped me through this journey. She has seen the good, the bad, and the imperfections of each of us. She has learned the right and the wrongs at an early age. I commend her and am proud of her. It is because of this strength she is willing to walk away in good conscious from the people and situations that do not serve her. She has learned to follow her heart and her gut. She can set boundaries on the behaviors she will not tolerate. This is an excellent quality of hers.

My daughter kept under the radar for many years, watching and learning from the other children in the family. She had many responsibilities she viewed as being more than she should have taken on. At the time, we viewed it as helping the family and everyone doing their part to work together. Everyone should work together! Her role sometimes was to take care of her stepbrother, a little more than she wanted to, was used to or could handle. I admit he was a handful for his parents and me, let alone an inexperienced child. Amid having to babysit him more, as any older sibling is sometimes needed, she lost part of her own childhood, and this was only her stepbrother, five years younger and a difficult child. Everything shifts from the youngest to the middle child, especially in a blended family. The struggle was real for her. I did not see this until we started therapy. There was a lot I did not see or realize.

My daughter is a very private person when it comes to her guarded emotions. When she got her tattoo, **"I am enough,"** at 18, I had my own interpretations of its meaning, despite not having a very personal conversation with her and sharing her feelings. I know at one point in my struggling relationship, my daughter asked me, "Why are Dalton and I not enough?" They truly were enough for me to love, and I love them both so much. There was something in my life lacking and trying to fill a void that had nothing to do with them. Unfortunately, they felt I was not picking them first. I wanted a happy relationship and happy kids, but deep inside, I was lonely. I didn't know how to fix it. I was grasping for the things that made me feel loved enough. When we do not feel loved enough, we blame ourselves, and our insecurities become heightened with fear. It was never about them not being enough for me to love them. It was me feeling I was not enough for anyone, especially myself. If I could return to just me and my two kids, I would have in a heartbeat. Life would have been different for all of us.

Many times, in a person's life they do not feel they are seen, heard or loved enough. They do not understand why someone rejects them or makes them feel that they are simply not enough to make someone else happy, especially when it comes to children of dysfunctional families. During our lifetime we all ponder the question, why am I not enough? We do not understand, it has nothing to do with us. Our values, beliefs and expectations of outcome are quite different. We forget to communicate our needs and just expect others to know. We will never be enough for some people because they do not know how to be enough for themselves. For some people we will be too much, as they do not know how to handle someone with such confidence and determination. We all show trust, confidence, understanding, commitment, and most of all LOVE in variable ways. Plus, we accept these things in diverse ways. Sometimes feeling judged, criticized, or unworthiness. There is so much communication lost during a love exchange if it is not the way we expected it through our expectations. Love and relationships get lost with the lack of the right love language.

Children sometimes feel they are not enough when there is chaos in the family. They wonder why their parents must fight and not be happy. The love of our children is amazing. There is no other feeling greater than that love. However, adults need adults to love very differently. We may not always make the right love choices in the end, but it's right for that moment. It is about what makes you feel the worthiness of love. It is not that we choose the other person over someone else, but we choose them to meet our needs differently. Sometimes, it even goes against our own values. We should not have to choose between loving one person over the other.

Everyone should feel as if they are accepted and loved "enough." If I could go back and change the way I reacted, responded, or listened, I would. There are so many lessons you skip over in a chapter till someday you are wise enough to understand them. Being enough and having enough are about the love and views you have about yourself.

I never realized our actual lack of communication until we started therapy. There was a lot of baggage that I did not acknowledge existed. She has a lot of triggers that create uncertainty in our relationship. A lot of distrust in comprehension and overall closeness. I can think back to several moments in the past when she needed her mom, and I was unavailable, either physically or emotionally. As she grew up, there were so many times I wanted to be there for her, yet her heart did not trust me enough to let me endure her pain. This gave me great agony. Feeling helpless is hard when you want so bad to be a part of their life. They shut you out based on their past doubts and expectation. I tried so hard to make it right over the past several years, to the point of taking every crumb of love I could get my hands on. I took in every moment she hugged me or spent time with me. I appreciated it all, no matter the cost. I went from being an unconscious parent in superhero mode to an over-conscious and lack of boundaries parent. I gave so much of my time, money, and energy into trying to build a relationship that I craved so bad. I wanted the kind of relationship every mother dreams of having with their daughter. I wanted to be her confidant, her mentor, and her friend. I longed for the bond between us to be strong. Hopefully, someday we can find our way to this.

All children go through stages of being independent with dependence. They crave their freedom of judgment, opinion, and time to create their own journey. Yet, at the same time, they trust that you will still be there when they need you the most. I can look back on my life and see how I created my journey at her age just the same. For me, I was travelling with an amusement ride carnival and enjoying my freedom without checking in with my mom. Only now, being in the same parental space, can I genuinely appreciate the longing for connection and the certainty of your children's safety. It is a scary feeling not knowing if your child is healthy or safe.

My daughter is at the age that she pushes me away; her supple ways still show me she needs me. She knows that when adversity happens, I will always have her back. I allow her to make the right choices on her journey for her, and I trust her and her decisions.

My daughter is my hero in many ways, just as I was a hero to my mom. We teach our daughters the strength of independence, to have a loving, nurturing heart, and a warrior's determination. Yet, in many ways, they will still always just be the princess in our heart. She is the one that steals the love of many just with her presence, and she shines toward the sun like a sunflower. We have raised our daughters like princesses and, therefore, teach them to straighten their crown as they become older. To keep going in the face of adversity and emotional upset, and to help others along the way even when you have nothing left to give. Life is about helping yourself and others. We sometimes do not teach them it is acceptable to be vulnerable during the times we struggle emotionally with life. It's normal to have hard days that we can barely help ourselves. We need to learn to regenerate ourselves. We exhaust ourselves and give more to others than we receive. We need to allow them to take time for self-care and feel acceptable about putting their needs before other people and their wants. We must take back our power and tell people, "Not today." We struggle with happiness when we give it all to others. We want others to give back to us the way we do them. Sometimes people do not have the same ability to love us or treat us the same way we do. This may be due to their upbringing and their own parents' lack of love, lack of empathy, or disconnection from them. We need to teach our daughters; it is okay to ask for help or walk away and find that person that brightens their day, and never settle for the life you think you deserve because you always deserve more.

Jade was such a strong girl growing up. I loved to watch her dress up like a princess, sing and dance. For years I enjoyed our mother-daughter time at her dance competitions. I loved being a part of it all and I remember many times I would sit in the crowd watching her. I would cry because I was so proud of her. Her determination, hard work, tenacity, and striving to achieve a goal were incredible to me. Jade has characteristics and a personality that makes others feel comfortable and safe with her. In grade 8, she received a well-deserved "caring and sharing the award." I am always proud to say that I am her mother.

As parents, we often feel distant in our relationship, especially as our children are trying to spread their wings, take on jobs, and create friendships and relationships while figuring out how to attend a school or start a life of reality by paying bills. They are no longer children dependent on their parents for everything. Both of my children are very independent like I was. She has two jobs, saving money and trying to balance her time. This is when parents get the short end of the time. They love us, but we are not a high-ranking priority of time. I get it; I was at her stage of life. But I long for the friendship with her someday of being able to share her life stories and her turning to me for guidance. I fear never having that time together to rebuild what was lost so many years ago.

We teach our children to have independence, then struggle with letting go of their dependence. Overall, as much as we struggle at letting go, we know we have done our job correctly. Currently, I watch my daughter create her own life and her own journey. I trust her process and know it is time for her to spread her wings and discover her own world. I wish we could be closer in many ways. In time, I hope we will have the relationship I have always wanted with her. I never try to force it, I just let her know I am always here. My door is always open.

*"**Give your children roots to come back to and wings to fly.**" Dalai Lama*

MY CHILDREN'S DAD

My children were only close to their dad for a few years; this is unfortunate. Their dad loved them very much and was proud of them. He made choices about his own life that took him down a different path than full-time fatherhood. The life he led was conducive to his own needs, not the responsibility of our kids. Although he tried to reconnect with each of them on several occasions, they had disconnected in their minds. Within the few years before he passed, they started to rebuild a relationship, each in their own way. We assume people should connect the same way we do, but we forget that we have diverse needs that must be met, just as our takeaway from a relationship with the same person is distinctive.

My children's dad and I were together for ten years. This relationship ended due to his gambling addiction. Their father and I did the best with what we knew. I encouraged a relationship between them to the best of my ability. My belief is that parents need to work together for the best interests of their children. We teach our children acceptance of others through the decision we make. Their father was able to be present in their life more towards the end as I became a partial bridge in rebuilding their relationship. I involved him in as much of their activities as I could. He and I supported one another and, in the end, remained friends. Our goal was to raise our children knowing that despite what happened in the past, it was to keep moving forward and not give up. I had great parental role models growing up. I consider myself fortunate that my parents could spend a Christmas dinner gathering for the sake of my brother and me, plus my children. I gave this gift to my own children. Thankfully, my partner was acceptable and even suggested this. We all worked together for the good of the children.

I did my best to support the relationship between the kids and their father for years, but I also realized it was not up to me. In the end, I struggled to keep my own relationship with each of them the way I expected and imagined it would be. They became the age of responsibility. Their choices of connection with their father were solely their choice. I reopened doors, and now it was their turn to step through it on their own. They were accountable for how they wanted their relationship, and how it would play out was now up to them. Leading up to the last few years prior to him passing away with Lung cancer, I would gently remind the children that their father was already on borrowed time. No matter what they decided, it would be what they would have to accept as their experience after he passed. I would like them not to have any regrets or resentments. No matter what the relationship is, we all carry some form of regret or resentment of what we think should have been. Sometimes our life choices sideline us so far away from our goal that we do not see the damage during it. By the time we realize it, we have collateral damage that we cannot repair, and then we leave our children feeling unworthy of our love or even their self-love. We never truly know how long we have someone in our life, so my theory is to make it count and never take the ones you love for granted.

Sometimes after people we love die or move away from our life, we grieve the loss of what we had but also what we should have had. Sometimes we remember life differently, more fun, loving, exciting and more connection than there really was. When we tell ourselves the same story long enough, we tend to believe the past to be any way we imagined we wanted it to be. We want to hold the special memories close. Acceptance in the grieving process is about understanding the role someone played in our life, knowing that whatever it was, they did the best they could. Everyone crosses our path for a reason. The reason was our marriage, so I could be blessed with two beautiful gifts of my wonderful, caring children. I appreciate it for what it was and the beautiful memories we shared. Your legacy will live through your children.

I appreciate the friendship that we had until he passed away. I remember having a very heartfelt conversation with him where we both confided in each other about all the mistakes we made in our parenting choices, our partners of choice, our guilt, and the love of our children. We respected one another, and our children were able to see that. In the final week, our children were by his bedside daily. It made me proud of them to see their love for their father finally come through. They knew in their hearts they were losing their father, and despite their differences, they loved and accepted him. They were hurting and would never get back the time they lost due to the grudges they held, the time we all take another person for granted being there, or just bad choices in life. I was also by his side the whole week, between packing, working, and moving. I wanted to be there for him, but mostly for my children. One of the greatest gifts, I believe, was a few nights before he passed away. Our daughter was present in the room when he told me he loved me. We all knew it was a different love, a respectful mother of our children kind of love. Love can only happen when you accept the other person for who they are and their role in your life. He knew I had been their sole provider, their biggest supporter, and despite every-thing we had gone through, we were friends, and he respected me.

Many people came to visit during his final week as he lay in the hospice. I know this was tough on him as he always felt left out and did not understand in his heart why everyone came to see him as he was dying. Many people like to assume they are more alone than they really are. My daughter Jade got a good laugh as she saw her dad rocking out with the air guitar. A sight I am sure she will always remember. He could tell the children how proud he was of each of them and apologize for his absence as a father. He realized his mistakes and was not as good as he thought he would have been as a father. He finally had the opportunity to share his gratitude and love with both of his children that week. In the moments when people are dying, they realize everything they missed and everything they regret. Others let go of all the hurt to just feel love and closeness at that time, and nothing else matters but love.

Their father was a hunter and an angler. As he lay in the hospice looking out one day, a fawn stopped outside his window. He got a glimpse and told everyone not to shoot it. Obviously, that never crossed anyone's mind. Knowing, watching, and waiting for someone you love to die is difficult. You think of what life should have or could have been with that person, plus each person has their own special memories to hold on to and remember.

The children were exhausted from a long night holding hands on their final night with their father. They knew in their hearts this was their final goodbye. As I drove to pick them up in the early morning, a fawn crossed my path in the middle of downtown, in the crossways of the four churches. My heart sank, and I said goodbye. I knew that it was time. It was a quiet ride home, as their children were both mentally and emotionally exhausted from their week. As soon as we reached home, I got the call. He was now at peace. I hugged each of my children as I told them the news. They were 21 and 17 when they lost their father. Very heartbreaking. The next day, they went off to be with his family for breakfast and the final goodbye, and I spent the day moving. A day I will never forget.

Just because a marriage does not last the way you anticipate it will, it does not mean you have to fight against each other. You loved each other once. You have children together. Love and accept that person for the beautiful gifts they gave you. Teach your children that you can always be respectful and kind despite your differences. You are their role models for healthy relationships.

Stepchildren

FROM MY 7-YEAR-OLD STEPSON, I learned time is valued. He struggles with focusing on tasks, especially when he does not enjoy something. I guess most of us are like that, so why do we expect a 7-year-old to get down to business when most adults struggle with the same thing? As adults, we call it procrastination or multitasking. As children, they get labeled ADHD (attention deficit hyperactivity disorder) when most times it is just kids who have more high energy than we do as adults and want to slow them down and extinguish their fire. They need to run their energy off and can just be kids. Time spent is precious. Seven-year old's need attention, someone to show they care and just have fun with them. Especially doing what they love to do at their level and their play. Take the time to do what kids want to do, and their interests are important. As adults, we need to adapt to our children just as we expect them to adapt to us. I remember amidst a power struggle of constant misbehavior, the thing he wanted most was for someone to just play with him. Just our time and focus. Something so simple. Children need to know they are important. The greatest thing we can give someone is *TIME*. Even as adults, we need that connection with others and the feeling we have worth to someone. We also need to learn with children the things that are most important to them are not to us, and vice versa. Watching youtube videos is the same as watching sports to us. A lost job to us is equivalent to a favorite lost toy to them. We forget that a child's perspective is different from that of an adult.

Sometimes adults or parents tend to give monetary or materialistic valued items instead of time. We feel this is a way to love yet get upset when it is not appreciated or valued to our expectations. We spend our time making money to buy items of value. If we gave our time instead, it would be valued longer at a greater price. In the end, all people really want is connection and time. It is the true antidote to loneliness.

As I watched this young child grow through the years, I saw many challenges he faced feeling like he is very seldom heard or seen. He craves the attention of others around him and will do whatever it takes to meet his need for certainty. He no longer has a stable home, living between his mother and his father. Most of his life has been chaos and a lack of understanding. Unfortunately, he has no stable male role model in his life to show him how to respect a woman, have financial responsibilities, or the ability to take struggles and make them challenges. He enjoys many things and has an incredible memory of the things he likes. Unfortunately, I see a very unhappy child. He seems like he is searching for love and acceptance, searching to be enough for someone.

This boy will always be my stepson in my heart, having raised him for the first 11 years of his life. He just turned 14, and with still a lot of uncertainty in his life, not much has changed. He still searches for love, affection, connection, structure, and acceptance. He is full of love and emotion. He needs balance, and commitment, as he gives up very quickly. Children become unregulated in their behavior and emotions when they are unbalanced and always shifting patterns without consistency. ***"As humans, we are hardwired for struggle, yet worthy of love and belong-***

ing," **Brene Brown.** When children must look for love and attention to have their needs met in any form, there is a feeling of disconnection. A lack of communication and understanding of "needs" creates a barrier to a happy and peaceful development. Once again, we realize that our parenting model shows them what we tolerate and how we want them to show up versus allowing them to be the person they are with acceptance and unconditional love. Boundaries with our children is a way of teaching them right from wrong, not teaching them they are wrong or bad. When we give our children our *TIME*, we show them they are important to us, that their thoughts and their visions are worthy of our attention. They can be authentic instead of training them to be who the world wants them to be or who we, as their parent, want them to be.

Just like any child, he is at a point of testing his waters and boundaries. He wants independence yet needs the guidance of an adult. His poor decisions of daily actions are creating his struggles within his blended family dynamic. He does not know how to get his needs met. So over time, the chaos builds till the damage is unrepairable. Each person is fighting their own cause, own boundaries, own trust, and own respect. Instead of fighting together for the cause, the breakdown becomes stressful and overwhelming for everyone. The young guy, now 14, has always doubted his ability in anything. He lacks self-confidence and is quick to give up. He is quick to undermine his own talents and discard or self-sabotage any great path he is on. Especially if the outcome does not lead in the direction of winning, he still creates a mentality that winning is the point of the game, no matter what you learned or the fun you had, regardless of the lessons he learned. It is all about the win because that is what makes you significant.

He was a part of my life for many years, yet, I had to remind myself that although I have the best intentions, he is not my child to raise. He has two parents that need to learn to work together and raise him to the best of their ability, even if it is not the best way. I had to step away to allow his parents to raise him and figure out his needs. He is not my responsibility. He knows he can always talk to me, trust me, and the door is open to visitors. This is how I will be able to support structure and boundaries in my life and stability in his. He has more respect for me than either of his parents. He has trusted in me that I will always be there. This is the love I have for him. I accept him just as he is. I understand his struggles and his challenges. This is his journey.

With my stepdaughter, I struggled very much. I enjoyed our conversations as if I was teaching her about life. We had a personality conflict due to our perspectives of things. She was introduced to an unusual way of life. This young girl grew up struggling for the attention of her parents. She was an only child with parents that struggled with their own relationships. Although they each loved their child very much, they had their own life and their own priorities. She grew up in a family-oriented environment but somehow got lost when she was no longer the center of attention. She had to fight harder for the attention of those that used to fight over her affection. Suddenly, she had a new brother, and her parents were separating only to find a stepfamily on either side within a brief period. It was hard to grasp not being number one anymore. In the new living arrangement, we both struggled to find our place and had many power struggles. She tried hard to fit in, but nothing felt like hers anymore. I don't blame her for her struggles. I can step back and realize that I was a part of the problem, not the solution. That is a challenging thing to admit and take ownership of. In the end, nobody won, and we both learned a few lessons along the way. I always see her as a person that was willing to go out of her way to please someone and enjoyed being helpful. She struggled with being alone and feeling unwanted or unimportant. She has matured and is learning that a job is beneficial for many reasons. Plus, finding the right peers is crucial to growing and figuring out your destination and journey. I believe she will find her path to greatness; she just needs time to love and believe in herself and find the things that make her happy. Her passion for life is the spark that drives her. I trust that this will be within the next few years. She has a good heart and a lot to offer but must learn to love herself unconditionally. Follow her own path, not that of those around her.

I have seen plenty of maturity growth through the years with my stepdaughter. I have watched her let go of the people she believed were heroes and release them from their pedestals, realizing that we are all human and everyone struggles with life's challenges. She has learned to set boundaries for herself and others and to allow her self-preservation. I believe as much as she wants independence and the ability to stand alone, this still feels like a challenge that she may one day conquer. She told me once that she would rather live with a homeless person than live alone. She wants to see the good in people and sometimes gives them too many chances. Most of us struggle with the same issues when we have a good kind heart. Unfortunately, with the love and attention she missed as a child, I still see her searching for love and acceptance from her parent. Her love for her parents is conditional on them meeting her needs, as she was raised to meet their needs. She was taught that when your needs are not met, it is ok to run, not deal with it, and not communicate it. Life is not always fair, and we do not always get our own way. In her maturity, she has learned it is best to communicate and set boundaries.

Both of my stepchildren had to learn to follow the rules, "do as I tell you when I tell you." Therefore, they both learned to "please" their father to get the attention they needed. He was the adult, he was right, even at times when he was not. Parents do their best to give advice or direction in what they feel is in the child's best interest or the situation based on their own upbringing, experience, or knowledge they have acquired. Children learn this behavior pattern and instruct their children or relationships in the same manner unless they break the cycle with strength and self-love. Most people go through the challenge of self-love at some phase in their life.

My stepdaughter, now 24, has become a mother of a baby girl. As she discovers a new path in life, parenting skills, and sleepless nights I pray she finds her way to love she deserves and happiness within herself. She has matured a long way to being an adult, and many lessons are ahead of her. I wish her the best.

Mother Guilt

MOTHER GUILT IS a real feeling that every mother struggles with. I cannot speak about fathers because I do not know what they feel. I would never want to assume their position with their children. Everyone has a sense of guilt from raising their own children. We all have *what ifs* about their future or past. We wish we would have been more present or raised our children differently throughout their years. Honestly, most of us are doing the best we can in the moment. Stress has a way of taking over and shifting our priorities from what we imagine our lives to be like to learn to survive in the chaos and reality of what life is like.

I had my share of mother guilt in every stage of my children's life. Sometimes I still punish myself for my past choices, just as my children may still blame me for the past. I have also heard my mother apologize for all the times she wished she had made better decisions, spent more time with me, or was not as sick as she was. This experience gave me independence that I passed on to my children. Most times we have no control over situations we feel past guilt for. The problem is we can never go back and change our past. We can only learn from our mistakes moving forward. We feel shame for the person we were as a parent and feel terrible for the relationships we had that may have harmed our children mentally or physically. At the time we did not understand why we chose those situations but found it a complicated process to leave. Somehow, we feel that the pain of being alone outweighs the pain we are in. We do not realize the damage it is creating at the moment and are unable to listen enough to understand. We simply think we are making the right decision at that moment in time.

Generational trauma is passed down. We do not always discuss it, and we want to be better parents than the situation we grew up in. Our parents had a more difficult life, and so did their parents. Abuse and neglect were normalized back 60 years ago. The older we get, the more we realize our parents were human and did the best they could with the knowledge and the skills they learned. Each generation adapts to a better life and passes on better values and beliefs. As parents, we want to give more and do more for our kids than we had in our own life. The older we get, the more we realize life happened, and it made you the person you are meant to be for your adulthood. As kids, we endured many life lessons that we did not realize we needed for our survival techniques as adults in our own relationships. We feel guilty for not listening and validating our children or making them feel like they were not enough in their world.

Children just want to be loved and have their basic needs met. When we give them too much, they learn to expect too much and lack appreciation. This leads to entitlement in many families. Unfortunately, in society today, children have way more than their lifestyle will be able to attain and maintain. Society has created a plateau of standard living that is beyond most people's means of affordability and creates an unrealistic look at life and financial entitlement. We have created a generation of always being entertained rather than learning to be bored. There is less ability to sit with mindfulness, problem solve and work through creativity in our mind by finding something to do or just taking at the moment. I know I gave my children the best that I had, and I see their gratitude which makes me proud. I had to work for everything I got, and so did they.

I know I did not always make the best decisions for my children in my relationship. I was doing what I thought was best for me in those moments. I believed they were not in physical harm and did not realize at the time the mental monsters they were fighting with inside their mind. We did not communicate our feelings or thoughts and failed to work together. As parents, we feel we have the right to make all the decisions without understanding how it affects others in the household. This is the reason so many children need therapy as adults. I had a threshold of a leaving point, and it was pushed to the edge many times. Unfortunately, I did not listen to my own intuition. As adults, we normalized some discipline, yet the situation became a fine line of abuse. The holding down vs. hitting them. It is all abuse. Sometimes all you can do is step back in fear. I knew internally that the next step was the last. That was my deal-breaker. Failed to realize that deal had been broken already.

The older I became, I realized through self-shadow work that I had toxic parenting traits. I always felt like I was in the middle of every situation. I just wanted to be loved. I would get so overwhelmed that I would turn to yell to get others to listen to me when I felt unheard. I did too much for everyone thinking it was good and easy instead of realizing it was enabling. I shared too many emotions, situations with my children, who were too young to understand adult relationships or life in general. I didn't know how to always be loving and validate my children, to see and hear them. Instead, I wanted the last word and to be right! I did not realize the trauma I caused, how this affected them at the time or the results later in their lives. I hope they know someday that I am sorry and try to be the best parent I know how to be. Parenting is a learning process.

I think as parents, we lose ourselves when we are in toxic relationships. We misplace our values and become desensitized to the world around us. We stop really paying attention to how our decisions affect the rest of the family. We only become concerned about what we want and think is right at the moment. Every child compares their upbringing to that of their peers, some have it worse, and some have it better. The world is changing its views and learning strategies for better parenting skills, as we have only learned our skills from the parenting we had. Each generation we learn how to parent better.

Children do not feel they are heard or seen growing up. They have a different perspective of their childhood both in their home and in their peer society. Now they have both social media and the physical world to pressure them into a feeling of belonging or hustling for their worthiness. They have teachers that listen and model a better way of communication and understanding than most of their parents. They lack communication and conscious parenting role models. Most do not have a proper example of relationships to learn from. I know my own children lacked the same proper relationship role modelling from my own relationships. We warn our children not to have the same type of dysfunctional relationship. Yet, we fail to model making the right decisions that create a better and more stable relationship moving forward.

Overall, despite my shortcomings and bad decisions, I did a wonderful job raising my children. We receive recognition as they grow and become responsible adults. I stayed in my toxic relationship with all the children. I did not realize the impact on my own children or how it would affect our relationship in years to come. I knew in my heart my children were protected, and despite my unconscious chaos, I knew I still had a breaking point. I sacrificed many of my dreams and goals to give my children the best I could in their life. More chaos happened when I was away from home, so I stopped leaving. I stopped taking courses and stayed home to protect, as my eyes were starting to open to all the red flags. I was not the best parent in life, but I was as good as possible.

I had to learn to forgive myself for the choices in the past. I forgave myself for all the times I fawned instead of fighting the situations. I forgave myself for not teaching my children proper communication, apologies, and validation of feelings. I wrote my children a letter of apology for all the issues I regretted or resented. They can choose to forgive me or not. That is their choice. Either way we cannot change the past, so I had to learn to let it go as a lesson for all of us. Overall, I was not that person anymore. I now know a better way to parent and lead. We are all different as we have gotten older. My children know my sacrifices, know my struggles and someday, they may respect my fight to become better.

After therapy and the letters to my children, I stopped apologizing. I stopped allowing the past or our emotions to make me feel guilty. I wanted to live, move forward stop holding on to things that I could no longer control. These were lessons for everyone, good or bad. Time to stop feeling sorry for myself and the decisions I made. Time to start living life again.

It doesn't matter the situation or the experiences in our life. People think they would make better decisions "if" they were in your shoes. I was the same but realized so many variables keep us stuck and not evolving in that situation. If you are not clear on your priorities, beliefs, and values, you will give it all up to meet your needs of love and connection.

Mother guilt is inevitable, but you do not have to shame yourself. Not everybody is doing their best, but sometimes that way of life is all they know. You can teach yourself a better way to parent consciously, communicate and love. No one is going to do the work for you. Get clear on your values and boundaries, so you can pass this knowledge on to your children. The best thing I did was learn to forgive myself for the past. I cannot change it, and I am not the same person or parent I was. Forgiveness for myself was an incredibility freeing from my past.

Forgive yourself and let it go.

The greatest gifts

THE GREATEST GIFTS are never bought or sold. They are *time and validation*. The things we cannot place a monetary value on are the ones we need and value the most. Understanding and acknowledging where I was in my life to now, realizing all the lessons life has taught me. I want to pass these on to my children without taking away their journey. I lived my life with love, heartache, challenges, and comebacks. I am a warrior and a survivor with everything that is in me. I will chase my dreams and keep rising stronger. That is who I am.

I had a key role model, a few good teachers, and a good support system. Most of all, I had the drive to succeed, the mindset to learn, and the heart to face adversity and come out living and loving stronger. I do not allow the world to make me bitter! I take it all, and it pushes me to be better.

We know we have succeeded in the real meaning of life when your children acknowledge your work as a parent and as their role models. Sometimes we do not think they are listening and learning, but they catch everything that falls. When your children finally tell you, "You are a good mom," something inside you releases all the mother guilt you have ever felt. A release of new energy, knowing everything you ever did or sacrificed, was worth the price of admission for that one statement alone.

Our children never want to admit they need their parents. They rely on us for knowledge and support. They want us to just be available when they need us at any time. I always figured my superhero power was to be a spider killer for my daughter. She hated spiders with a passion. She would wake me up at any time of night to kill them. To me, it did not matter how old she was because it was the last thing she admitted she needed me to do for her. They do not like to admit how much they rely on us until they are older and on their own. As parents, we are taken for granted regularly, not on purpose but just as fulfilling their needs.

As our children grow up, they realize that as parents, we did the best we could. We were just learning at the same time they were learning. What works for one child does not work for another. But the greatest gifts are when you realize that they grew up with a better understanding of life and independence, even when you were uncertain of their journey or your own. We learn that we just need to trust in their ability and their decisions to make the right choices. We are not their only role models in life. They will take a little from each person they met on their journey. This will create their beliefs and characteristics to make them the person they grow up to be. When you look at your children and know they are good people with great values, ethics, and standards, you know you succeeded as a parent.

We all just want our children to be happy, but it is a great gift when in return, they care about your happiness in life and love. The greatest gift is forgiveness of who you were in the past and acceptance of who you are now as a parent. The understanding that nobody stays the same. We all change, and we all grow through our different experiences and lessons.

Values and Beliefs

We learn Values based on our family dynamics and our belief systems growing up. Then our peers start shifting us with the ideas that they have from their family. When you hear something long enough or loud enough, you tend to believe it to be true, despite the truth behind it. This is usually passed down through generations until someone breaks the cycle of belief. If you believe everything in your life has to be a struggle, it will be because that is your belief. Think of life as challenging and overcoming the obstacles as rewarding. The language you choose is important to your belief system. Most people struggle with believing they are "enough" because they were not loved or cared for with respect or their parents were unable to be the person they needed or wanted. You can change that belief at any point by knowing that it was never about you. It was about the person that did not know or understand how to love or care for you. They were in their own life struggles and did not know how to love or care for themselves at that point in time. It is generational trauma passed down.

We start to open to a new world of vision and possibilities. As we start to explore the world around us, we see opportunities to expand our knowledge. Then as we experience life, we change and adapt our values to what we feel is right or wrong. Deciding what works and feels good versus what we do not like and feels uncomfortable. Then we rate our values against our own priorities in life, which also shifts with age and relevance. The values we have in our 20's and their priorities shift with our values in our 40's, 50's and 60's.

I learned through my own relationships and experience what felt good or did not. My core values are communication, integrity, and respect. For me, these go hand in hand. When you say you will do something, follow-through is important as it is the cornerstone of setting boundaries. Communication or lack of it can make or break any relationship. People fall into assumptions and tell themselves a story rather than getting clear on wants, needs and overall issues. Respect is about both. Most people want respect but fail to give it to others the way they want to receive it. My perception of respect may have a different standard than yours.

At some point in our life, we have all had the feeling of not being good enough for someone to love. I did until I realized that I was the only one rejecting me. What a revelation when we realize we are in control of our thoughts and can tell ourselves a different story and change our beliefs. When people do not feel enough, they blame themselves for their own shortcomings or think something is wrong with me. We are our own worse critics and judge ourselves harder than anyone. We struggle when we feel rejected or abandoned, especially after someone tells us they love us. Sometimes people grow apart, and their values and goals no longer align for the future. You can still have love. It is just a different love than before.

We have basic needs; Love and connection, significance, certainty and uncertainty (variety), growth and contribution. We need all these at contrasting times and at varying levels of our lives to keep us balanced. Our needs change as we accomplish our goals and satisfy our needs. If you are unsure of your needs, you may look for the wrong answers and search for the wrong goals. *" **The world***

will give you whatever you ask for, so ask wisely, and you shall receive." …. Tony Robbins.

Values help determine your wants and needs and be able to set healthy boundaries. When we do not communicate our values, we get enmeshed in someone else's and forget to set boundaries around them. We lose sight of what is important to us and in our life. Most people will give up their values to meet their needs regardless of the consequences or the relevance of the healthy versus unhealthy. Your worth is, so you never let anyone undervalue you. You know what you deserve and can walk away from situations that dimmish that or make you feel unworthy.

I realized before any relationship. You need to know four things: your values, your worth, your boundaries and your deal-breakers.

Boundaries are important in any relationship or friendship. You can be generous and still have boundaries. Deal breakers are about knowing your values and worth, yet having the ability to walk away despite love because trust or integrity has been broken. Deal breakers help you to leave a situation, yet also help to give your relationship a standard to which another person is supposed to uphold. Communicating these four things in a relationship creates transparency, and your partner knows where you stand. You must be willing to follow through with the consequences of your standards. Otherwise, you will overlook many red flags and find it difficult to leave. This is usually what happens in a codependent and enabling environment.

Authentic, Empowered and Connected

I STARTED a journey a few years ago about changing my perspectives. I was struggling with many things in my life. All answers come to you when you ask. A life coach came to me for my profession, and in turn, we helped each other. Nothing happens by accident. I have had these experiences many times in my life, and I am open to understanding it. My life coach guided me on a journey of examining me... as I am the only person that can control my thoughts, emotions, and life. It takes a long time and many more challenges of daily life to be changed. I had thought it was my job to make everyone happy, and healthy and balance everyone else's life. I was the MOM, and it was my job to teach the kids lessons, including saving them from everything and everyone. I had to learn I was on my own purpose and journey, and so were they. Adapting to a new way of thinking has been difficult and challenging.

Authentic.... *is about being the best me at any given time. Not about being anyone that someone else wants me to be. Not requiring anyone else to be different than they are. "To Thine own self be true!" (William Shakespeare) Listen to your heart and it will guide you.*

Empowered... *Having the right to stand up for yourself, the* *right to say NO and walk away from anything you do not agree with. You can choose to walk away from anything in life that you are not happy with. No one must allow themselves to be in a place of discomfort. We teach people how to treat us. So always be yourself and know you have a choice to stay or walk away.*

Connected... *A feeling of belonging to anything that you desire, feeling safe in your space. Love makes us feel significantly connected to another human being (or animal). The loyalty and the need to give to something or someone more than yourself.*

I am learning you can have all three of these aspects in your life. This gives us the personal strength to grow!

Authenticity is how we show up in the world, with others and in our environment of pleasure, work, and home.

How do you show up? Are you different in one group vs. another? Who are you on your own vs. with others?

People will judge you no matter what you say or do. Most times they are passing judgement based only on the parts of you that they see or upon their own values and beliefs. We never show anyone all of who we are; therefore, we are different from everyone.

When you are feeling fear based on other people's opinions, remember two things:

1. **Other people's opinions of you are none of your business** (Opinions are like assholes... everyone has one)
2. **Why do you care?** - when judging others or allowing other people's opinions to bother you, dig deeper into your own emotions of what is a deeper connection. How does it affect your life?

To be authentic, Remember the phrase **"to thine own self**

be true" usually, who you are alone is your true authentic self. Acceptance of yourself in your space to just be you.

You do not need validation from others. You are enough exactly as you are. Everyone has two needs.

- **To be seen -** the right people will see your love and kindness.
- **To be heard** - we all want people to listen and understand Us, NOT to fix us.

This truest gift is the ability to simply hold space for yourself and others on their journey.

The less we judge others, the less we judge ourselves and vice versa. Let go of perfection, and appreciate your imperfections. They are beautiful and belong only to you.

Be present, live with purpose, and love yourself worthy.

Having Authenticity in my life is learning how to show up regularly for myself and others around me. I no longer care what others think. I understand everyone has their own opinions based on their own life experiences. I realize that just because I can give or receive a suggestion does not mean I have to take it. I do not need to have to explain my choices in my life. I realize that you may or may not like me, and I am okay with that! We will never like everyone we meet. Acceptance and love come from within, not from hustling for your worthiness. No one can make you feel inferior without your consent. This is based on your interpretation of their judgement.

Empowerment in my life has allowed me to use my voice for good, not create chaos and control. I can set boundaries and walk away from people and places that no longer serve my present or my future. I cannot control my past; I can only take lessons from it. I learned to stop enabling others and allow them to be responsible for their own decisions and consequences in their life. I understand that I completely control the voices in my head. I have the power to shift my thoughts and my mindset and create my own resiliency based on my experience and my acceptance.

The true antidote to loneliness is connection. We all need a connection to someone or something. It makes us feel wanted, needed, appreciated, and loved. It is important to be alone and be able to love yourself and connect with yourself. This allows for a deeper connection with others. You feel grateful for them in your life without feeling that they need to create your happiness. You are completely alone but sharing yourself with others helps to give them and you both comfort and connection. You learn and share your joy, experiences, and laughter. Someone to share your excitement and your fears. Connections are important to get us back to our hearts and out of our heads.

Love and Relationships

When we first meet someone, we only see what they want us to see and what we allow ourselves to see. We become so infatuated with the thought of someone caring for us and accepting us into their life. Someone whom we feel is putting an effort into us. We put others on pedestals just as they do us. Things change over time, and we feel the other person has changed, but we are just seeing the whole person, the good, the bad and the ugly. We all have those sides. To genuinely love is to accept a person when you get to know them, the whole of them. This may take several years as people do change over the years. We all grow, and our acceptance of things we initially tolerated changes. We learn more about ourselves and realize we have boundaries, values, and ethics. A true partner who loves you will encourage you and support your growth, ambitions, and passions. Look for a partner who wants to learn about your goals, plans, and future. They will not stand in your way; they will encourage you and believe in you when life is tough. Yes, Life is tough... but you are tougher... and the challenges only make you realize you can take control and go for it to the best of your ability. Love takes patience, acceptance, trust, communication, and the ability to compromise. This is for loving yourself and all others. We need more acceptance of ourselves and others. This allows each of us to be the person we are meant to be. We need to bring out the best in one another by being the best YOU.

When choosing to love someone, you love them for all they are, despite their shortcomings you find amusing in the beginning. After a while, these issues become annoying and intolerable. Now is the true test of loving unconditionally. It is not about giving up everything you are but allowing someone to be who they are, just as you are. Acceptance and understanding are the biggest challenges you will face at this point in time. Your partner has characteristics in them that you buried inside of you for a reason. At first, you think it is awesome because it is written that opposites attract; therefore, they are everything you are not at this moment. Together you find that level place. In fact, like attracts like. People like people that are like them. There is an ebb and flow between the attraction of opposites vs. the same. You want someone with the same values, goals, and dreams, an excellent work ethic, and positive characteristics and attitude. Yet you also need them to have enough variety that you do not mirror images, and no one can motivate or balance the other. Balance is a great key to a successful relationship.

Every relationship needs boundaries. Testing these boundaries can be challenging in any relationship. You need to understand that your partner's actions and behaviors have nothing to do with you. Most times it is a reaction out of emotion, as emotion is the driving force of any human being. People only react when it affects them emotionally. Sometimes it is the wrong emotion that is driving them to react. Lack of perspective is the cause of that. Most couples can love one another if the situation is perfect, with no illness and no hardships financially or emotionally. When you test the waters, and things get rough, the ones who really LOVE are those who find a way through anything, still willing to give with everything they have. Two people who choose to live together need to remember that there will be disagreements as they both have different values and beliefs. Each was raised differently, parented differently, and lived their lives differently. All those differences shaped each of you to the way you live your life now, right, or wrong. Not everyone will agree all the time. We are not our partner's boss, parent, or child. As a partner or spouse, you accept the person wholeheartedly. Our role as a partner is to give them love, understanding, respect and allow them to be the person they choose to be. If you decide this person does not follow your values or beliefs.... you have the right to choose to walk away. It is okay to leave when a person does not suit your life anymore. It is not okay to hold on to someone just because it is convenient.

Understanding the difference between men and women is a key element in lasting relationships. We are different. As John Gray explained in the book "Men are from Mars, women are from Venus," men are described as rubber bands. When stretched to their limit in a relationship, they pull away for their time, they hide in a cave, whether emotionally or physically, they are just not available. The more women chase men, the more men think women are insecure. This would be true in the case when women are in the wave cycle when we feel unworthy and need to be reassured that we are just as desirable as we once were. Women need attention and reassurance all the time. Women tend to give to all of those around them, expecting someone to give the same things back someday. Both men and women ideally just want to be needed and appreciated. When you love someone unconditionally, you learn to appreciate the cycles of people and embrace them rather than be afraid of them.

Our roles change throughout our relationship. In the beginning we may have taken on more of a His and Her duties or did so much through people pleasing or love. One person becomes the house cleaner, the cook, the caregiver, and more, while the other person does half if any. Eventually, the dynamic wears thin, and one person feels they do everything. They are left feeling unappreciated and even used somedays. Sometimes we want to change the game's rules in the relationship and then fail to tell the other person the situation no longer works. Many factors play into this. Hours of work schedule, kids' activities and over exhaustion. Find a new solution together. Do not become resentful with expectations of the other person picking up slack if you never ask for help. Communicate your new needs and find a way to make them work, if possible. In a relationship, usually, one person is done before the other even realizes the first was unhappy. Ultimatums come at the end, usually not respectfully, which concludes the relationship.

When we dwell on the problems or issues of another person, we usually tend to overlook the fact that it is our problem, not theirs. Other people are typically happy doing what they are doing. It makes them happy. We have expectations that we have created, a certain way we want them to respond or act according to us. And when they do not fulfill our needs, it frustrates us, and we demand change instead of allowing them to be themselves. We have the choice to walk away. So why don't we? We try to control the people in our life to fulfill a need for certainty or significance. Accepting others wholeheartedly means we must accept ourselves wholeheartedly, which for most of us is the hardest task to fulfill. We are our biggest critics! It is easier to judge and blame others because it takes away from the real issues we have with ourselves.

When you choose a partner, remember there is no perfection in any of us. Therefore no perfection in any relationship. In the beginning we tend to put people on a pedestal, but pedestals break and crumble. We want to believe the other person is going to stay that perfect forever. We never want to see them for the person they truly are. They are the person that showed you all their strengths and some of their weaknesses. The real trust comes when they feel safe enough to show you all their strengths and weaknesses. A shift in a relationship happens when you start to see their strengths as their weakness. They have been the same person you fell in love with, but how you see them is different. What happened? You forgot to see their weaknesses as strengths. You forget to allow them to just be themselves and, no matter what, allow your acceptance of them. That is truly unconditional LOVE. To love someone, to accept them for all they are. It is not about changing them but loving them so much that you trust them enough to do and be the person they are. Loving someone unconditionally does not mean you have to love everything about them. You still have a choice to create your own boundaries of acceptability.

It is important to honor someone else just as they are. Whether it is our children, our parents, or a spouse. Everyone in your life is there for a reason, do not change them. If they want to change, that choice is up to them. If they become incompatible with your life, you have the choice to walk away. Take ownership of the choices in your life.

Change happens when we aspire to be the best person we are. Sometimes it takes others to show us a new direction in life, separate from the life we know. People take us to new levels that sometimes we cannot accomplish by ourselves as we have different life experiences. It takes the support of others, a direction of passion, and a purpose in our life. We are challenged to separate the addictions, misguided directions, and toxic people from our lives and learn to be with the people who bring out the best through support and understanding.

When we live our life a certain way, we create standards and beliefs. We think every one must be this way and therefore have expectations in relationships. Then you meet someone you think has the attributes you are looking for but later discover it is a mask. Below the surface, they have their own pain and trauma that has made them unkind, cruel, and narcissistic. We want so badly to believe in the good version of that person that we continue to push aside the hurt, anger, and unwanted experiences they give us. We develop patterns in relationships with the same toxicity, thinking the next one will be better. We try to fix others to show them a better way or teach them to grow or change. All these moments in life are just experiences that make us into the person we will be. We finally realize what is acceptable and what is not. We re-learn our values and create new beliefs out of each experience. In a-ha moment one day, I asked myself, "why was the person not getting the lesson?" At that moment I realized that I was the person that was supposed to get that lesson... not them. We create a belief that is all about others learning lessons and other people changing. We must be perfect. I love me. So, it must be them.

Life and everything in it is all about beliefs and perspectives. Five people can be taught the same idea, and each learns a different lesson. We forget life is about perception and how we perceive things in our own mind, based on experience, motivational state, and emotional state. Just as we perceive it one way does not mean that is how it was meant. People tend to react based on emotion as that is the driving force in anything we do, good or bad. We do things for pleasure or pain. When we shift our perception, we can see life from another person's point of view is to be empathetic. The problem is we do not know their values and beliefs to understand exactly their point of view, so we now place assumptions about what we think they feel. When you learn to shift your perception, you learn that the difficult things now seem small by accepting others as they are. We learn to stop dwelling on the things that make us mad and just realize how minor it now is. When we stop taking everything in life so personally, we understand that people's actions really have nothing to do with us. If we were to remove ourselves from the equation, they would still be the same person. Part of healing is not feeling drained in someone's presence. You can love that person, trust that person and be in the moment with that person. But learn to walk away from anything you do not like or that makes you feel uncomfortable. No one ever forces you to stay. You always have a choice.

Through my relationships I have learned more about myself than living by myself. Each relationship taught me; my standards, beliefs, personal values, and what I need from others. I understand Self-respect, and everything that is important to me. I learned that I need security and shared priorities and values. I realized after working so much that I was not living and that I did have goals. I discovered that although we create "our expectations" of people, it is based on a standard of values we hold. I learned that loving unconditionally does not have to mean losing yourself for the sake of loving someone else. Unconditional love doesn't mean unconditional trust or tolerance. I learned that resentment builds a stronger will, and life gives you choices, so move on. We are only as strong or as weak as we allow ourselves to be.

The healing has shown me a better way to be in a more loving and compassionate relationship. I still catch myself in stories I tell myself through some triggers that I realize are usually just in my mind. It is amazing when we are conscious of our thoughts and how we can control them. When we learn to heal our past, we can have better relationships with everyone around us. We learn to take nothing personal in life. That we have no control over anyone else. That we do things out of love, not fear. That we start to communicate and listen from a place of understanding in the relationship and can become united in goals.

When we learn to heal our past and start loving ourselves, we realize we are completely without anyone else. Everyone else in our life is just a bonus of happiness. That toxicity falls to the floor, and it no longer affects us the way we once allowed it to. We stopped feeling anger and frustration over the things that did not go our way. We start appreciating life's moments and start living life more passionately.

People tend to make relationships harder than they are. They want the other person to fulfill all their needs that have never been met, and they want the other person to love them more than they love themselves. You are meant to love yourself the most. *You are enough alone.*

A relationship with the right person will bring you joy without fighting for attention. It is about having tough conversations about values, boundaries, and deal breakers. These three are my go-to when sharing relationship advice with anyone. It is funny how we never realized the importance of clarity on these key points for any relationship in our life. But most of us were taught values based on our family values, not our own. We adapted as we learned about others' beliefs or values from those close to us. We were not taught boundaries other than personal space. We wanted to please everyone, so we were afraid to upset and walk away. We were taught to keep our parents happy... or else. So, we grew up with many codependency traits that we later try to undue through setting values and boundaries. Then we can create our list of deal breakers. Most of these were learned the hard way through relationships that ended badly. Most couples forget the toughest conversation of all. What if it ends? No one wants to think of their relationship ending, but it may. Too many people have issues with children and custody or splitting of assets when everything is over. No one wins, and most times, it is only the children that suffer through the hands of adults' greed and ego. Transparency is the key to communication with relationships. If you want honesty and trust in your relationship, it starts with you. Anything you omit or fail to disclose is not honest. Respect is about being seen and heard in any relationship. You may not always agree with the other person but always be willing to listen and compromise. You are partners in love and life.

When we heal from our past relationships, we learn to take ownership of the part we played. We give less blame to others, and we feel less shame about our choices and the way life is. We understand we cannot go back and fix it or change it, so we learn to accept it as it was. A learning experience. Every relationship will show you about yourself and what you want to evolve in any relationship. Take the lessons and move on. Free yourself and celebrate your new growth. Honor your values and allow the other person to find the person better suited for their happiness. It is okay to outgrow a person or a relationship. The only person you are meant to love forever is *you*.

Most people that seek a relationship want to know the outcome before it starts. They go into it with the expectation that they need to know how long it will last. They have a need to give it status and a time frame. The best relationships I have started were from a place of no expectations. Every relationship has an expiration date, so enjoy it for what it is as long as it is. It will give you the lessons or the love that you need to meet your goals or your needs at the moment. It could be a transitional relationship or a whole new chapter. You do not know the ending before you read the book, or you would never read it. This is the same as relationships. Everyone is different, and each chapter will provide you with a new lesson in your life. This is your life, and you get to write your own chapters and change the ending at any time.

Everyone searches for the perfect relationship yet has no clue what it looks or feels like. They think they want a romantic comedy or love story that shows the perfect ending. Yet they settle for what they think they deserve because of their own understanding of what a true relationship should be. Most children grow up without two loving parental figures that teach them respect, love, communication, or how a good relationship is formed or needed to survive. Then we wonder why we have such a tough time finding the right person or even being the right person. We do not know how until we have had several bad relationships that teach us the values we seek later in life. It is a never-ending cycle. We think we are supposed to be the perfect partner and do everything to make them happy. We eventually figure out it is about making ourselves happy and not needing anyone to complete us. We are completely alone, and it is up to us to make ourselves happy.

Relationships are about working on yourself to be a better person than who you were in the relationship before. We all have lessons to learn and take ownership from. Love is not selfish, and it is not about keeping score. Relationships do not have to be challenging work, but they do have to have communication and understanding. Communication can be challenging if you do not know how to do it. Relationships are about working together for your future and your goals.

Lost in the Shadows

Close your eyes and imagine a world full of love, fullness, excitement, and wonder. Feels perfect to be happy and in love. Then everything changed...slowly. Sometimes we do not realize the changes in love that happen so slowly; we accept what is going on. We adjust our love to become more forgiving and more tolerant of what is happening. Our life becomes unmanageable and yet fall to the blame of someone else. We feel like we have roots and cannot move. We try to stand our ground and make excuses for the behavior, yet we do not leave.

Slowly you slip away from your values, the people you were once connected to, the things you used to do, and most of all, your own happiness. It feels like you got lost in the shadows so quickly, but in fact, it took years to figure out that you have already been there for years. Lost in the shadows of hope, despair, chaos, and destruction. You fall into a dark hole and are not sure how to get out, the walls start to close, and you feel trapped.

Only you can choose how long you stay in the shadows or trapped in the dark hole. You can capture all the people you want to be trapped with you or simply decide when you have had enough.

Break the chains, fight off the demons and claw your way to the surface. Do it from Fear. Do it from Love. Just do it. Figure out your drive. Love yourself enough to fight for all you have. All you have is you. Choose happiness and get out of the shadows, for this is your life to lead. Believe in yourself. Then when it is all over... Let it go. Give forgiveness to free your soul. Holding on to resentment, will continue to keep your heart and soul trapped and lost in the shadows. Peace and serenity can only come from a place of surrender.

Therapy was what I needed most at a desperate time in my life. My life was in chaos, and I felt like everything was spiraling downwards with no up in sight. My ex-partner had gone through years of up and down in his own state between depression, binge alcoholism, pot addiction and narcissism. No one was happy in my household, especially me. I knew I needed a change, but I was lost and no matter how many people told me how. I wanted to keep trying to make it right and the way it was in the beginning. It never happened! We think everything will work out but never know HOW or WHEN.

The question is, how much do you have to sacrifice to make someone else happy when you are not happy yourself?
We think if we love them more, they will change and be the person they were when we first met them, but they never are. Once we start to see the true colors in someone, we need to learn to walk away, not give up our own life to save someone else. Or make it work when we are the only ones "fixing or dealing with the issues."

I was in a bit of a shame spiral, not wanting to go to Al anon. Thinking I got this, I am strong and resilient. But we all have a breaking point. I reached mine and started therapy. After a few thousand dollars in therapy sessions, I realized I was not the problem. No one was. I just never saw the signs of mental abuse. He just could not love me or be the person I once loved. I unmasked the real him, not the one who is hidden by alcohol all the rest of his years.

Therapy reminded me of how strong and capable I am. It gave me a voice to speak up and see the truth. We all need a therapist or a coach that pushes us to see and speak the truth.

Most people would rather spend their money on other priorities, but remember your mental health is the best priority, and only you oversee that. If you are going through it, chances are someone else must. You are never alone unless you choose to go through it alone. It is okay to ask for help. It does not mean you are weak. It just means you need support.

My experiences have taught me – *Never stay anywhere that makes you uncomfortable or unhappy.*

We all have a chapter on shadows, skeletons in the closet, or all the stuff we are not proud to say we did, or a lifestyle of choices. It was not the best time or the best decision in our life. It turned chaotic or just very unconscious of the life we were living. But some of those bad decisions in our life turned out to be the greatest decisions of our life as well. The shadows feel like demons clawing you back or taking you down into a black hole. Keeping you trapped instead of moving forward. We see no way out from the shadows. Everybody's shadows are different, or how long we allow them to maintain their grip on us. Some people hold on to their shadows for a long time and hold it as trauma. We need to stop chasing our shadows of doubt or fear and just let them fade into the past. Their job was simply to test us and give us lessons we were meant to learn and could not do any other way.

Let the shadows fade, let them go, thank them for the lessons, and give forgiveness to yourself or others in the shadows.

Separating from my Identity

We were all born with the identity of being someone's child. We were born authentic, yet as we started to take on our parents' values and belief systems, we started to change and adapt to our environment. We were no longer taught how to think for ourselves, as we were unsure of right and wrong, so we were told. As children, we believed words and few actions. Eventually, we start to take our own values or beliefs or that of our peers. We allow judgement of ourselves or hurtful words from others to penetrate and pierce our worth. We start losing our authenticity to feel we belong to something more worthy of ourselves. We believe in others more than we believe in ourselves.

We turn to people pleasing, trying to make our parents happy and calm. We try to be the perfect child thinking the reward of love will be enough. We lose our authenticity to become someone we think others want us to be. We try harder to fit in, yet sometimes the harder we try, the more bullied we feel. Children can be mean as they are all searching for someone to love and have a connection with. Unfortunately, all they know is how they were raised. Attention is still attention, no matter what.

The older we become, the more we seek validation in our emotions, thoughts, and beliefs. We start to learn that when our beliefs are different from our parents or we were raised differently than other people in our peer group, we compare our life to others. Feeling not good enough to be loved because our parents did not sacrifice their happiness for ours or make us feel like we were constantly number one. We never realized they only did the best they knew at the moment. We all make bad decisions. We attach our identity to other people, groups, or who we think we must be and, in return, sacrifice our identity and our authenticity. We always believe that when others had it easier or more money, they must have been loved more if they got their own way. Sometimes life is a matter of circumstances, and the challenge is not to lose our way.

Authenticity is about not allowing yourself to get bogged down by judgement of others. When we chase an identity, we give in to others' perceptions of what we should be. We allow other people's opinions to decide what we like to listen to, dress like sports we play or watch, who our friends are and what we think our future career should be. We allow the values and beliefs of other people to over-rule us through emotions. We try to make everyone happy by being the person they want us to be rather than who we are, which makes us happy.

When we become mothers, we carry a fortitude of identities. For many years, we have lost our authenticity in trying to be the best mom, partner, caregiver, cook, taxi, teacher, and friend. The truth is we cannot sustain those identities and still be true to ourselves. We do not know how. Most women didn't grow up having the best role models for parenthood, partner selection, and relationships.

AUTHENTICITY is the need to be yourself and express who you are and what you feel. Unfortunately, these needs are also part of your survival that got lost in your childhood. As children, we need attachment for survival. As we grow older, we rely more on attachment and will give up our authenticity to feel a connection to fulfill our needs. When we unconsciously fail to allow others to be themselves, express themselves and feel what they feel, they start to suppress and ignore their truth.

This is the cycle we are trying to change. Your parents did it to you, and you subconsciously did it to your children. We suppress what we fear or what is new or indifferent. When you are unable to convey who you are and what you feel or express what you want or need to anyone, fear takes over. You give up your authenticity for the feeling of attachment and belonging. You may meet your needs of love, connection and belonging but lack authenticity.

Some people struggle with not being real or authentic because they suppress their gut feelings and emotions. Numbing emotions may manifest in addiction and physical and mental health issues. You cannot selectively numb your emotions. When you no longer know who you are, it is difficult to understand what you enjoy or even feel pure joy. It is challenging to follow your path or purpose until you find your authentic self and stop trying to belong to the wrong people.

Who you give your attention to accounts for how you feel at the end of the day. When we give 10% of our best self to the people that support us and 90% to the dysfunctional relationships in our life, we feel depleted. This can lead to burnout. Flip it- give 90% of yourself to your biggest supporters and 10% of your effort and time to those that drain you if you must have a relationship with them. Be able to set Boundaries. Listen to your gut feelings when it is time to step away.

Learning to be authentic and separate yourself from your past identity is a challenge. But eventually, you reach the age where other people's opinions or judgements are no longer important. You have had enough lifetime experiences to know what you like and what works for you. You are clear on your own values, beliefs, goals, boundaries, and deal breakers. Listen closely to your heart, and it will guide you through life. If you make a mistake that will happen anyway, take ownership and change direction. You are only stuck in your identity if you continue to search for belonging and fitting in, rather than self-acceptance and authenticity.

Self-Sabotage

Sometimes we directly or indirectly look for a way out of a situation. We create a pattern of self-sabotage. We tell ourselves a story to make us feel better. We give up trying or pretend to. Sometimes we tell ourselves people will not miss us, then do everything possible to make that happen. We have created a situation that we do not understand. When things happen in relationships that we struggle to deal with, it is because we do not feel the situation will change. We start to give up, believing there is no way out but to look for a reason.

Many people self-sabotage and never realize they are doing it. Addictions are a huge defeat. In this case, we tell ourselves we cannot or do not want to live without it. We feel it is a choice. Constantly, with addictions, it takes away from the good by giving what you think is good now, but that moment does not last forever. It becomes a search to fill the void of seeking pleasure over pain until it creates more pain than pleasure. If you want the good moments to last, pick the people or things that will give you lifetime happiness. Moments in time can fade and be forgotten. We can tell ourselves any story we want. It is our journey. Look back on your life and all the things that were going amazing. How and why did it change? Many times, it is because we tell ourselves we do not deserve " that person", "the situation" or continually question "why does everything bad keeps happening". But you have made all the decisions to lead you to the place you are now. It is never anyone else's fault. Your limited beliefs have played the largest role in your decisions you feel are self-sabotage. In fact, your goals or values just did not align with the actions you were willing to take. If you do not like it, rewrite your story, shift your thoughts, and pursue your dreams. After all, anything is possible if you try. You are what you believe. If you believe you have nothing and no one will miss you, chances are you are not believing in yourself and not giving someone a reason to miss you. You are sabotaging yourself, your relationships and everything. If you do not like yourself, why would anyone else? Finances are another self-sabotage; we tell ourselves we cannot afford things or we are struggling to stay above the water. However, we put ourselves there. Sometimes we have no choice at the moment. How you choose to move forward and get up or get out is up to you. Just because something bad or unfavorable happens does not mean you have to unpack and live in that moment forever. With everything in life, you have a choice. So, with any situation, ask yourself; what did I do to cause or create this and now, what am I going to do about it?

We forebode joy, and we sabotage our thoughts before we allow moments to happen. We think of the worst-case scenarios prior to waiting on the outcome. We do not think we are worthy of happiness, fame, money, or successful life. We allow fear to define our direction and choices in life. We settle for a life we have rather than a life we desire. We do not follow our hearts in case we fail yet fail the attempt by not trying. We decide that we are incapable of certain things yet never give them a chance.

Addictions

ADDICTION IS a harmful disease that destroys lives, relationships, and future. Unfortunately, we do not see the harm until it is too late. When people have addictions of any sort, it is because that addiction fulfills a need. It is up to them to understand the need and want to change the habit, and no amount of disapproval from anyone will change the behavior. We all develop childhood attachments, control, deprivation, or rejection. Any of these attachment issues can develop into addictions. Addictions can also be relationship behavior. When we try to control someone in any relationship, it always becomes a power struggle, and subconsciously we continue to seek that in all relationships. We become controlling because we think it is easier to take over than to accept what is or fight over what should be. But sometimes, we will fight for what we believe rather than listen to options, reasons, and experiences. This is when our ego takes over. It is about what is important to us, not always realizing the extent of harm and hurt it causes any relation. This is our life to experience as we need to as it is our journey. We forget to take advice and adjust. We forget that other people's lessons can also be ours, and sometimes we do not need to experience them ourselves.

Listening to others supplies us with an opportunity to decipher what we learn by listening to the experience and doing it for ourselves. Everyone learns differently. We have a challenging time understanding that not everyone will conform to our expectations in life. Everyone has an addiction. Sometimes, we just do not recognize it or take ownership of it. EGO says there is no problem. Remember, it is hard to change ourselves and even harder to change someone else. Be with someone you trust and honor... life is a give and take.

I have had a few patterned relationships with partners with addiction. Gambling, drinking and drugs which lead to cheating, lies and manipulation. I was blinded in the beginning but usually had control and strength to walk away until the one relationship became my addiction. I struggled with the need for love. I thought I had found it. I thought this time was different until I lost myself in the addiction of love.

Addiction can become the mistress of an affair in a relationship. It takes over and becomes the focus of your wants, desires and even your identity. Addiction will trick you into believing that you need it more than your family, your money and any relationship that was ever important to you. It takes away from your time, your passion, and your growth. It makes you believe it is the only way to survive and fill the void of emotion without ever dealing with life. Unfortunately, life has a way of eventually catching up with good or adverse consequences. Natural consequences are the most heartbreaking as you realize the people that you fought so hard against were the ones that really loved you the most. Sometimes when people with addictions cannot fight their own demons, they lose themselves to mental health or just take their own life. Watching the people you love struggle with this disease is very heartbreaking. You realize there is no way to help them; only they can find their way out of the dark hole that keeps their soul trapped.

As a child, I had a lot of "pain" associated mentally with alcohol and addictions. I watched people fight and argue that were otherwise civil and loving when not intoxicated. I realized that it shifted people and their personalities to an unrecognizable or uncontrollable state at a certain point. I learned I had no power over anyone in that state, and all I could do was watch helplessly as chaos unfolded. This paralyzed me in a fawn state with my own life circumstances as I started feeling helpless in many situations with my own children. I knew from the past you never argue with a drunk or step in their path as they become fearless with being 10 feet tall and bulletproof. Sometimes you must allow a situation to play out and hope for the best. I have many regrets about my inability to protect my children when they needed me most. Although it is no excuse, I have forgiven myself for my unconscious ability to seek good choices and decisions and to leave an unhealthy, harmful relationship. Like most women that get caught up with someone with addictions, we realize there is yin and yang. You remember why you fell in love and that reason is the power that keeps you hypnotized for years, like a casted spell.

When you fall in love with someone with an addiction or that is narcissistic, there is a lot of cognitive dissonance within the relationship, and you fight with yourself about the separatism of feelings. You know that the person has a good, kind, loving part to them. Yet, they can become disrespectful, hurtful, and self-absorbed. You have difficulty understanding how it can be the same person. Your mind always takes you back to the good person and the good times. It hates to think and accept that you picked this person that was not in alignment with what you genuinely wanted in a partner. You allowed them to take over your values and beliefs to the point of making you feel helpless in many situations. Afraid to speak up and afraid to stand up.

A person with alcohol or drug addiction will not realize the pain of their judgment or the harm they cause others emotionally, if not physically. It is like another entity takes over and creates a whole new persona of personalities. This is why many people with an addiction are also on a spectrum of mental disorders. They become

"Dr. Jekyll and Mr. Hyde." Sometimes alcohol or drugs can calm you down, or increase your level of awareness, heighten your energy, or sink you low. You can be confident, feel like you are superhuman, and then be nasty and aggressive. Whatever your true nature is, the mask it will reveal. Over time and circumstances, addiction will make you believe it is your only friend, and it will have you choose it over your family, friends, your job, and anything else that used to be a priority. It will suck you in if you let it. It will lead you astray with no regrets or remorse, and everyone is left to wonder how to help. Addiction is a long and lonely path, especially when it gets your mind to play along. Sometimes when you think you think you understand and are at the point of no return, you hit bottom, then you learn you can always create a new rock bottom.

If you ever get the chance to break free from its evil clasps and find new meaning and priority in your life, you need to stay away. For many, a gnawing inside of you comes occasionally knocking to see if you missed it. With everything that happened, you have a lot of amending to lead a peaceful life. "You walked 10,000 steps in the forest; you must walk 10,000 back out to find your way back." These were the lessons my ex-partner learned in rehab.

I would never choose to love a person with addictions, just as someone never chooses to have addictions. Sometimes in life, things happen that take us beyond our own thoughts and our own out-of-control behaviors. Most people do not know they are stuck in the middle of addiction until it is too late to pull themselves back out. By that time, so much of their life has become chaotic, unmanageable, and lost. This also happens to the family that once loved them.

Addiction taught me to set boundaries, take time for self-care, and have grace and compassion for myself and someone suffering from addiction. Addiction taught me acceptance, the ability to let go of the part of my ego that constantly felt rejection. The ability to let go of all the expectations of the entitlements we create in life. Addiction taught me to love myself first, unconditionally and make myself happy. That is my responsibility, and my choice is how I carry out that.

At some point in our life, we all fall on the spectrum of addiction which we deny is an addiction. By Gabor Mate's definition, ***"Addiction is manifested in any behavior that a person craves, finds temporary relief or pleasure in but suffers negative consequences because of, and yet has difficulty giving up. In brief: craving, relief, pleasure, suffering, impaired control."*** Addiction is anything from caffeine to cell phones. There are addictions that we feel are not harmful because we enjoy them, and it is not hurt anyone else. However, in the long-term, cell phones are just as detrimental to your health and the relationships around you as drugs or alcohol. They diminish your social abilities. People will spend all day on their computers or cell phones, yet it is usually not an all-day process if a person drinks or does drugs. Once they hit that threshold, they fall asleep. Unlike cell phones that keep you coming back, there is no end cap. Addictions are strongly associated with mental health. Talk to a therapist, take control of your mind, and your mental health will be so much better, plus less probability of long-term disproportionate addictions.

When we are trying to detach from someone else's behavior, we also need to detach from our own nagging behaviors. *Nagging is a counterfeit power*. It allows us the false disposition of still being in control. Telling someone what they should do or how they should do it takes the focus away from our own goals and journey and puts the focus on the person we may be in a relationship with. We need to set boundaries for ourselves as well as others. This is part of learning what our responsibilities are.

Just because they may not do it your way does not mean they are incapable of doing it. Letting go is about allowing others to face their own consequences for their decisions and their actions.

When we get to a point where we can just accept someone in their addiction, we learn to manage our expectations and let go of trying to fix anyone or change them. We lose the initial force that drew us together as we start to see the person in a different realm than we did in the first place. We know they have demons that we cannot help them fight. We learn that sometimes we just need to walk away and allow them their journey. As we let go, we start to connect with ourselves, pay attention to our needs, and let go of trying to fulfill someone else's. When you love someone that suffers from addiction, it is difficult to end the relationship because you have been enmeshed in it so long that you have an addiction to that person. Letting go comes with a lot of grief and hurt. You feel a deep sense of betrayal for believing in them. Letting go is about honoring yourself. It is about loving yourself through the journey of all the stages of grief until you reach acceptance. You know that person will never return to the person they were before the mask came off. You will never see that person the way they were. All you will see is pain within the person and the relationship as you believed it was supposed to be or was at one point.

Addiction is a Disease! Everyone in the addict's life, including the addict, suffers at some point in their disease. You want the addict to seek help for themselves somewhere along the journey. You want them to want a better life for themselves and their family. All you can do is support them, love them, and accept that their journey is on them, no matter their choices or consequences.

Frog in the Water

"IF YOU PUT _a frog in boiling water, it will immediately jump out, knowing it will be hurt or killed, but when you put a frog in tepid water and slowly turn up the heat, it does not realize the danger. It slowly dies." -_ Stephenie Meyer

I was this frog; I did not see the harm my relationship was doing to my mental health. I was losing myself for the sake of loving someone else so much throughout my codependency phase. I did not see the chaos it was creating or the dysfunction in my family. I did not want to believe that this relationship I felt so good in was the same one that always made me so frustrated and unloved. When we get caught up in helping someone live their dream, we forget about our own. We get lost in loving and making others happy and lose sight of our happiness. I normalized the fact that segregation was happening. We were all busy doing our own thing. In fact, we were just falling apart. I normalized and hid my emotions of rejection from my kids or my partner. I did not see all the red flags that were in front of me. I did not want to. When the relationship was good, it felt really good. It felt amazing for the first five years, but I missed all the signs and red flags of this relationship, so it kept me in a false sense of security. I learned to accept ownership in my part of the relationship. I was codependent, and he had narcissistic traits. After a few years of researching and rediscovering myself again, I changed my life and created my own happiness. I was able to break free from my codependent behaviors.

I was the frog in the tepid water, loving a narcissist with many struggles and red flags that I saw but overlooked in denial until it was too late. They start off with love bombing and putting you high on that pedestal, making you believe you have found your soulmate. Through love bombing and endless compliments, they entice you to fall in love with them, to get what they need or want from you and the relationship. Slowly everything changes, and you start to see lots of red flags, but because they are great in other areas, you dismiss them. Mental abuse and devaluation are the next steps. They devalue you in many ways and manipulate you to fulfill their needs. They gaslight you through a grooming process of simple phrases that make you doubt yourself or your reality. I never saw the abuse, the manipulation, or the gaslighting till I started researching.

At the start of our relationship, no one had heard of the term "narcissist," but it was not as prevalent as it is today. Many people are on the spectrum with characteristic traits of a narcissist, but only a trained professional can diagnose a narcissist. Many people need this quality trait to be as successful as they are in their life.

It wasn't until after we moved that I decided I needed to change the boundaries and expectations of our relationship. This made his narcissistic characteristics more apparent. I knew he always focused on himself or turned every conversation back to him. I knew he had to have all the attention or everything he wanted. I was naïve and just accepted this was his personality. The kids were not so accepting of his behavior. I stipulated that he was responsible for half of everything financially. This was new for him, as I enabled many aspects of our relationship and accepted crumbs to pay the bills before. He would take his share out of his paycheck, and I would get the rest. This never covered half or the extra I had covered for his car and other desires or habits. I was starting to set boundaries, and he didn't like it.

After six months into our new move, his addictions started to take over. At least this time he recognized it. But it also gave him an excuse out of the relationship, leaving me in extra debt. He didn't care. This was about him. He went to his sisters for a few months and then to rehab. At least that part was a blessing. He went through suicidal thoughts and a stay at the mental hospital, which was not his first or last stay. When things got tough, this was his way out of reality and responsibility. Through all this, I stuck by his side, even though it meant I was running on empty. I did what I could to get by. Every day I felt broken and lost. I was lonely, and even though it was not a great relationship anymore, it still filled the void of companionship. I convinced myself there was still potential in the relationship I wanted instead of the reality I was living. That is why most people stay in this type of relationship longer than they should.

After five months of his absence, he returned to the area, but on his sister's suggestion, we had different living arrangements. This was the beginning of the end. I had our house, which he abandoned, and he rented a one-room apartment. He still lives there, three years after the fact, it is all he can afford, being on a disability pension. At certain times, his son has shared this one-room apartment. No space for either of them. That is their choice. He created a life where he can get by on the bare minimum and does not have any more responsibilities than necessary. At this point, I knew our relationship was over and had run its course. Our values and goals were no longer aligned. During his first year in his apartment we dated, it was intriguing at first, but it was back to the love bombing stage again. Over time I realized it was not the same relationship and never would be. As he returned to work, got back into pot, and started lying to me again, I felt like less of a priority in his life, and we drifted apart. He tried his manipulation, but it did not work this time. I had become educated with strong boundaries.

Once again, he became manic. His life went into a tailspin. This happens when narcissists try to take the focus off what is really going on. So that the empath refocuses their attention on the person in trouble and away from their own healing. It happened many times in our relationship, I just never understood it till now. I had a therapist that guided me through the process of leaving and understanding my relationship with the alcoholic narcissist. This was my addiction pattern I had to break because it was taking a toll on my own mental health and spilling over into several areas of my life. I sold my house, turned down his marriage proposal, and started to see the game unfold. It was like the cycle of abuse was on fast forward. They do this, so you feel like you are the crazy one in the relationship. He talked in riddles, and life was a puzzle. He said he loved me and was afraid of losing me; the next moment, he yelled and belittled me. I finally saw the monster the kids did all these years. I had enough! I could finally see the patterns of his narcissistic behaviors.

For most of our relationship I blamed the alcohol addiction, but after several conversations, I realized it was the narcissist behind the mask. Once you unmask the narcissist and discover their game, they quickly discard you. Leaving you wondering why I was targeted and how I got through all these withdrawals of the narcissist symptoms. It is a roller coaster ride of loneliness, fear, rage, denial, confusion, and relief. It takes a long time to heal after a breakup with a narcissist. Focus your healing on yourself and remind yourself of all the bad shit that happened. My best healing remedy was to write him a thank you letter. I thanked him for all he had taught me, both good and bad. People with narcissistic behaviors also have good qualities, and you have good times and bad. That is why it is hard to comprehend the whole relationship, and it leaves you feeling betrayed and empty.

Usually, others can see the frog slowly being harmed or dying before we, the frog, can see or feel it ourselves or even want to admit it. They see the ripples in the water and the boiling points being raised. Sometimes we just choose not to see it, normalizing the situation. At this point the relationship and the person still meet some of our needs. For others, it is simply the fear of leaving or being alone. We know and understand the chaos in which we live and tolerate. We do not know what life outside our chaotic world brings with new challenges. We fear we will never be loved more than we are or feel this is as good as it gets. We tell ourselves a huge story of why we need to stay in this toxic, dysfunctional relationship. We think the other person will not survive or live without us due to mental or financial limitations. We become enablers! Trying to make everyone happy, we become a part of the problem instead of the solution. We now accept and tolerate behaviors we would never have prior to this relationship. Narcissists and addicts pick people that are enablers and codependent yet strong and independent. Typically, it is in the empath lonely phase that the charm persuades us of the narcissist's personality. Eventually, we give up our values and meet our need for love and connection. Even if we have been strong in our past, they have a charismatic way of molding us into who they want us to be. Therefore, we quickly lose sight of our boundaries and values and give them what they want. When people start suggesting their concerns in our relationship, we need to step back and ask more questions. We need to look at the red flags and understand they are coming from a place of concern. If your children are not happy, ask yourself why. Better yet, ask them Why.

We need to learn what side of the rope we are on. At some point in a codependent relationship with an addict or someone with narcissistic patterns you realize that you are drowning. One end has the narcissist, the cement block, at the bottom of the lake, and you are holding the buoy at the top. The only way you can free yourself is to cut the rope from the person or thing that is holding you back and swim. Sometimes this is our own mindset, limiting beliefs, or past trauma. As soon as you cut the rope and start swimming, you have regained control of your life.

It is up to you how long you stay feeling helpless and hopeless in your life. Most people will put themselves in a position allowing others to have financial control, which can also lead to mental control. You feel like you have nothing of your own value. Therefore, it diminishes your self-worth. When you have nothing, you feel like nothing. Learning to cut the rope from a partner or anyone you are not growing with, supporting you or giving you respect can be challenging. It can feel easier to keep treading water, but eventually, you lose your energy, lose your breath, and drown. The longer you live with your head just above the water, the longer it will take to learn to swim with confidence. Cutting the rope is the first step in taking back your life.

UNMASKING THE NARCISSIST

The narcissist wears a mask,
From the first day that you meet.
They are charming and charismatic
They are the center of attention.
Love bombing and intense emotional connection.

You become enmeshed within each other
You lose all sight of your values and your goals.
You lose your identity of who you were and who you are.
The addiction of the relationship is strong and purposeful.
You are entrapped within the cycles and patterns, looking to escape.

As you unmask the narcissist you will see the true person.
A Narcissist does not love themselves.

They are incapable of loving someone else.
They will manipulate, gaslight and belittle you.
They are full of entitlement and control.

As you unmask the narcissist, you will never see them the same.
All the red flags become visible and difficult to hide.
You learn to be one step ahead of the narcissist and the game they play.
You learn to recognize the behavior and the signs.
You learn to take back your self-esteem and your worth.

Goodbye Codependency

WHAT IS CO-DEPENDENCY?

The codependent enabler in any relationship struggles with.

- The need to fix someone or their situation
- Cover up situations
- Manages someone else's emotions
- Taking on someone else's feelings or behaviors
- Focuses on the other person's needs or wants before
  your own

I know you may not want to admit it, but you have an addiction. It affects your self-worth and creates a toxic, unhealthy environment and relationships. It is a silent addiction that sometimes you hate to admit or brush off as nothing.

- The giving of yourself more than receiving.
- The complaining of doing more than your fair share
  after you have allowed someone to overstep their
  responsibilities.

- The times you said yes, to someone when you wanted to say no.
- The moments you watched all your values crash because you thought love was worth it.
- All the red flags you missed because you saw potential in believing.
- All the nagging you did try to control a situation you had no control over.
- Each time you gave up your dream to live someone else's dream.
- Each time you allowed someone to manipulate and control what you did or your choices.
- Each time you shrugged off your toxic behavior or failed to take ownership of the part you played.
- Every time you felt drained from someone else's behavior or choices, that had nothing to do with you.
- Every time you walked on eggs shells or kept the peace instead of walking away.
- Every time you let someone else control your emotions rather than make yourself happy.
- Every time you gave in because it was easier than fighting for what you believed.
- Every time you enabled someone, knowing they can do it themselves.
- Every time you made the choice not to allow someone to feel the consequences of their decisions or actions.

Codependency is as much of an addiction as any of them. But the struggle is real.

90 % of codependency comes from childhood trauma and our parents' patterning. It was built on a reward system of "doing what you are told to." It stems from seeking love and validation from a

parent you may not have otherwise received if you were not making them "Happy."

When you grow up, you seek to make others happy and fall into a people-pleasing pattern by enabling them and giving more than you receive. In the end this results in resistance, regret, and resentment.

It usually starts in childhood and can be generational. But you have the choice to change your future. You have the right to heal and recover. The first step is admitting your addiction.

Once I learned boundaries, my life changed. I stopped enabling others so they would like or love me. I started allowing others to problem solve and fix themselves. I learned to be **BRAVE** and created my new life based on that principle. I created **Boundaries** that were suitable for me and my relationships. Understand my **Responsibilities** in my relationships and do not take on what is not mine. Be **Authentic** in my life and have acceptance for who I am with acceptance of who others are. You will never be happy trying to fit in, not being yourself. Know your **Values,** from that you can set your standards, your boundaries and create the relationships you want. Live life through **Empowerment,** let go of enabling patterns that keep us stuck and learn to empower others. I created a course to share with others.

I did not realize how far into codependency I was until I lived with an alcoholic with narcissistic behavior tendencies. I lost myself and the only way out was to create Boundaries. An addict and a narcissist are only happy when you are enabling them. There is a blame game that goes hand in hand with that toxic relationship. Then the relationship becomes an addiction. It's difficult to leave the pattern of a relationship until you become strong enough to learn the abuse cycle, set boundaries, know your worth and leave. Most people stay longer in the relationship because they remember and want all the "good times" back. But once you unmask the truth of the relationship, you will never feel the same about that person again. So, the only thing to do is make yourself healthy enough to love yourself worthy of a better life. This is your *responsibility*. You will never change another person, but you can do your own recovery work, so you do not get into the same patterns of relationships. Most people never do the recovery work and deal with their own shadows and therefore repeat the same lessons or patterns with new partners.

Finally, I can say, "I am not codependent." I broke my pattern through recognition and self-work. I can give generously within my boundaries. I give from a place of love with fewer expectations on investment return. I have standards and values within my relationship and am willing to walk away when love is not enough. I do things because that is who I am, but I will not accept a one-sided relationship either. I need a partner that gives because of Love, not expectation. Equality looks different in each relationship, and if both people are happy, it works for them. All anyone really wants is to feel loved and appreciated for what they do. Not be ruled by someone's happiness being your driving force to do things.

I know I got this codependency trait from my mother. Sometimes I see it in the things she says or does. She needs to make others happy and comfortable or feel like she should do more, yet she feels helpless. She has come a long way, as we both have. I do things now because it makes me happy, and I enjoy it. They are happy in return, but I no longer feel obligated to make someone happy. That is the difference with codependence.

Mental Health

As I GO through and refer to mental health as a spectrum, I am only relating to one of my own experiences. Watching someone, I loved to diminish mentally into depression and then manic. (Please note I am not referring to any of the disassociated spectrum health disorders or diseases.)

My perspective on mental health issues is we all have a choice on the story we hold on to in our heads. We decide on our emotions and how long we want to hold onto our issues that we created from our expectations we set for others and ourselves. We may not have gotten to choose the story of our past, but we are still responsible for the choices we made in our own life due to the circumstances. We are responsible for our healing, our recovery, our discovery, and our own growth. We must take accountability for our choices, how we treat others, our addiction choices, or the ways we choose to avoid our own learning to adapt and understand the why of our life. We need to understand that someone's opinion of us is just that ... someone else's opinion. No one thinks the way we do, nor have they endured our life. We all handle situations differently, including grief and trauma. No one can measure their life compared to someone else's life experience. Pain is inevitable, but suffering is a choice. We can choose to isolate or choose to open and communicate. Self-talk keeps us from experiencing life and relationships to our fullest potential. We get caught up in never measuring up because we create a life that we can never measure up to.

The biggest lesson I learned about (depression and manic) mental health was that no matter what we feel or think someone else in anxiety should feel or do, it is not up to us to judge, change, fix, or do things for them. This behavior only creates a stuck behavior. Instead, learn to sit in their silence and be at peace with yourself so you can be at peace with them. Learn to detach with love from the person they were or the person you want them to be. Love them harder in their moments of silence. Show up and be seen because a person in depression cannot understand some things clearly. They cannot hear the music and understand the laughter. So, do not expect a friend with depression to come searching for you when they need to talk. Search for them, listen to their silence, and show up for them in a way you never have.

I know many people with mental health issues have no control over their behavior, thoughts, patterns, and state. There are many ways to seek help with and without medication, but it takes being responsible for yourself enough to deal with many of your past shadows or trauma. Some people need medication to settle their brain activity and balance their chemicals.

So many young people commit suicide from getting stuck in their stories of today or the past. They get wrapped up in the story of the past, which cannot be controlled or changed. They become trapped by the emotional obstruction in their head of not knowing or believing there is a way out of the NOW feelings. There is always a way out. They get stuck on the same human fear that we all have, that we are not enough and therefore will never be loved enough. This is all perspective. Sometimes we just do not want to accept the love in front of us. Our ego wants to love the way we expect it to be.

Some people are incapable of giving it to us in a way to meet our needs.

My firsthand experience with mental health and depression was with my ex-partner of 11 years. I thought we had a great relationship overall. We had so many things in common and really enjoyed each other's company. I thought we were soulmates. When I first met him, he had a self-confidence about him that shined. He had everyone's attention when he entered a room. It was like he demanded it but in an effective way. He was friendly, approachable, funny, and overall, a good guy. He struggled with the unknown addiction to alcohol but was naïve to his own problem. Slowly the cockiness turned to arrogance. He lost his job due to alcohol, and he faded slowly. In a passing conversation, he mentioned past depression issues, and I thought nothing of it, having never experienced anything like this before myself. It is a whole new world watching someone slip into depression within their own head. Their mental thoughts start to control their every thought, emotion, and physical state. He became lost in his own mind. Random thoughts of paranoia would creep in, hearing voices that make you want to do unspeakable things to those he loved the most. He felt alone, yet I was always there watching over him. Watching him slowly settle into the comfort of the discomfort of his life. No ambition, no goals, no compelling future. Unsure of what today was even supposed to bring as every day turned into the next.

Although I felt helpless in helping him, I had to keep the family and myself above water. I went into survival mode, with all the coping mechanisms I had within my reach. It became automatic to focus life on everyone else around me. Our four kids needed their mom, but as time went on, I became unconscious of my everyday patterns. It is like we tend to cater to the person that needs us the most, and the rest must fend for themselves. Overall, it makes everyone more independent, which is important later in life. I forgot about my own needs. I put myself last, and I started to lose myself. It is hard not to allow yourself to be sucked into someone else's depression. Thankfully, I was able to pull myself out quickly as I started a course of self-improvement and seeing perspectives in a whole new light.

As my partner faded with his mental health, I remember the terrible feeling inside of me that he was not to be left alone. So, after him spending the day with his parents, we decided he needed to be admitted to the hospital. Unfortunately, they do not admit someone until you feel suicidal. So, a few days later, we were back again to admit him. This is the biggest failure in our local mental health system. The second is they do not have therapy for trauma when you are in it. They manage you with medication, just enough to put you back on track to a maintenance state of mediocre living, knowing they have created your lifestyle.

His mental health and depression episodes started in his early 20s, and he has been medicated off and on for this, but never once did anyone care about the trauma behind the addiction or the mental health. Most people with mental health issues will numb themselves, leaving them feeling helpless and hopeless. They create a mask to cover their pain. This can last years, and some people around them will never know the true person behind the mask.

Eventually, he balanced out again and found new passions and a new spark. Until the alcohol got in the way again. Responsibilities of life became too much to handle, and eventually, he was back to depression, and his suicidal thoughts were at their peak as he finally realized he was an alcoholic, and he felt he had betrayed himself and hurt his family. He was in a state of feeling unworthy of living and be loved. A lot had happened with our family dynamics over ten years to bring him to this point of helplessness and despair feeling, including some family history that crashed into his memories resulting in guilt and shame. When people hold trauma based on guilt and shame, they move into their head instead of their heart.

They have difficulty releasing it and letting it go to a place of forgiveness and acceptance.

As my partner recovered with medication and connection with others through his addiction treatment center, we found our way back to love for a brief time. I had never stopped believing or loving him through all the difficulties. No matter what curve ball was thrown at me, I was in this relationship. Deep inside, I knew I had more lessons I needed to learn. At the time, I thought my love for him was unconditional. I now realize if he was the person I had met years before, it was unconditional. As it turned out, my love for him was conditional. I loved him if he fit into my box of conditions. These were my sense of values and beliefs about what a relationship should be. Life changes and people uncover their masks, or we discover some of our values and goals. We had shifted to a different plateau of life; I was in a healing state that was different than his. We are no longer aligned. It is okay to walk away from someone to save your own mental health; you do not owe anyone an explanation for the choices you make in your life or on your journey.

The only way back from loneliness and despair is through connection. His time at the addiction center showed him he was not alone and that everyone has their own struggles and challenges with addiction. It is about your spectrum and the willingness to be vulnerable to ask for help. His life of sobriety has taken him through many hardships and challenges. At first, it was easy and manageable. Then once again he found himself at the hands of longing for connection, which took him down the slippery slope of bad decisions and wrong encounters. He stayed away from alcohol, but marijuana was his choice. Although, in the past, he used it as a proper sleeping antidote and it worked graciously, the side effect was the decreased time spent with loved ones. As he slowly reconnected with a social bond, the cycle started with deceit, lack of integrity and then complete loss of control. He went from a sleeping remedy with marijuana to a creative strain. His body overloaded. His mind, thoughts, emotions, and behaviors went out of control. His life became unmanageable in a way I had never seen before. This strain of marijuana changed his personality till he became manic, vindictive, and extremely narcissistic. He always was on the narcissist spectrum, but never to this rapid fire. It brought out all his worst qualities to the extreme. We went from a good loving relationship with communication and growth to a crashing halt. Looking back, I can see the charade of anger, deceit, and broken promises. He became a monster.

The children saw this side of him, and I had failed to fully understand and accept in the past, knowing a deeper part of his soul. The manipulation, control and gaslighting put me at a threshold where my mental health was becoming a concern. His abusive nature at this point was starting to worry my family and his. I felt I had given 110% for our relationship and thought, "this was my return on investment?" Time to have a breakthrough! I had already been studying human behavior for the past six years. Getting my power back with each passing episode meant to break me but only made me more of a warrior. I had to learn I was fighting for the wrong thing. You can only fight for love when both are willing to put in the effort. It never leads to long-lasting success if one person does all the work.

In his manic episode, his narcissistic behavior side lasted several weeks. Growing intensely with the vast trauma that surrounded him. We both went into our own survival coping mechanisms. His was bullying and mentally abusive. I went from feeling rejection to empowering my warrior. Finally, my warrior saved me. He ended up in the hospital after a crash of insomnia and constant unconscious mania. Sometimes in my mind, I wonder if all of it was real or a game. Too many things fell into alignment of timing. It was like a well-laid plan of a narcissist that had just been found out. As I watched him over the next few weeks, I felt as if he was planning his suicide. He dropped off his children's belongings, and he had me delete him from my social media, like he had no existence. He was mean and spiteful, making others hate him. When he crashed, he had threatened his ex-wife regarding their son and ransacked his own apartment. Finally, the police came, and he was admitted to the hospital. After six weeks and different medication, socialism, routines, and fulfillment of his childhood needs attended to, he leveled out. Deep inside me, I knew this was not the end. I increased my own boundaries to protect myself and my mental health. I was finally able to end our relationship, I was done with the mental abuse. This whole episode made it easier. On top of this, I was dealing with moving and my ex-husband dying. No wonder I felt exhausted.

My role changed as I healed and let go of my anger. As a friend, I continued to check in on him regularly, take him to psychiatrist's appointments and help him with the necessary steps to receive a disability pension, as he could no longer work at this point. Over the next few months, I learned many lessons about myself, mental health, and addictions. I did a lot of shadow work during this time, so I could heal and not let this toxicity drain me.

I learned that each depression or manic episode is different and that most of them are triggered by trauma, the unwillingness to seek therapy, and learned helplessness. You cannot help people who do not want to help themselves because they get their needs met by being in that state, and it is difficult to pull them out. But I also learned it is particularly important to not take someone else's state personally or reflect on what you are doing to help them. I learned to let go of my ego and honor my own mental health by doing check-in for him, yet not staying too long to be drawn into the void of emptiness. Although we drifted far away from the couple we were many years before. I learned to sit in his silence and hug the emptiness that overtook his soul. He was so focused on the past regrets and the unexpected future that was being made by his decisions and choices. Yet, he could not seem to find his way to the gratitude at the moment. He would stare blankly at the tv for hours, feeling helpless, not caring, worried and unable to sleep or eat. At this moment it was so difficult for him to see how life could be better. He could not just get out of the state as everything was very unconscious. Over the weeks, I slowly watched him crash again and stop taking medication. Several times I mentioned to his psychiatrist about therapy, not just medication. My theory was we needed to find the root of the problem. Through a few therapy sessions with my counselor and our countless conversations, I knew he had some deep-rooted issues or trauma with his family. Yet, the remedy always falls back on medication for maintenance. This provides stability and sustainability enough to allow people with depression to slip back into their comfort zone.

After a brief period, my gut instinct responded to the crash he was experiencing but would not take accountability for. I saw the weight loss, insomnia, lack of appetite, and blank stares and despite his doctor's best medication efforts, it was not enough to save him from being trapped inside his own mind. Unfortunately, you cannot admit someone to a hospital because of self-neglect and you know they are in depression and fading quickly. The rules state someone must be of self-harm or harm to others. This is one reason our suicide rates are high. This is something that needs to change if we are going to change the stigma around mental health. Allow people to go to the hospital and talk to someone or stay a few days to balance themselves out when they know they are crashing before it is too late. He was lucky this time. I followed my gut instinct and showed up to realize he had taken 90 sleeping pills. Thankfully, all other addictions had ceased the year before. Otherwise, it could have been lethal for him. That day, I saved his life. I am not a hero; I am a friend.

Every day he improves, but without therapy for the past trauma, regrets or resentments, or even a compelling future, he will remain chained to his depression until he is willing to escape the stories in his head. He does not live with gratitude or go after his dreams. He does not want to take accountability for his future or his past through recovery therapy. So, for now, he is stuck in a repetitive life with no joy, happiness, fulfillment, or goals. Therefore, depression lasts a long time in people that are not motivated to change. Eventually, people in that mental state surrender to the void of darkness or isolation, whatever that looks and feels like to them. Three years later, he is in the same situation he was after we parted ways. No job, no money, no car, no future! It is a sad reality when people choose to do less than the bare minimum to survive. Depression makes you slowly die a lonely life. In the end, only he can choose to change.

We are still acquaintances, with a one-sided lean, which has ended now that I have found new happiness in my life. I did my part to help him out after he lost everything in his life. My only response to the people that ask why? Two reasons: because I can, and because I would hope someone would do it for me if I were in that same situation. I have no expectations of a return in any way. I have no invested interest, and my ego no longer controls the part of me that once felt entitled to measure trade. Out of these years of love and hardship, I found my voice, my values, learned to set boundaries, and the understanding of my role, especially when it came to ego, enabling, and co-dependency. I learned to forgive myself and others. I learned what loving someone else unconditionally truly meant. At one point, I loved him with all my heart. I was willing to sacrifice it all. My love was limitless at that time. I do not respect his behaviors, and our values are not aligned. We took each other to a deeper level of the person we were meant to be. I am a wiser me for everything I learned because of that relationship. Unfortunately, he is stuck in a position of uncomfortable comfort. He lost his passion for life, his hobbies and his love. Slowly he is finding a new way in life, and we are only in vague connection. He now has his family support, despite their minimal contact. The hardest pill to swallow was realizing he was incapable of loving me (or anyone). I finally saw the man behind the mask and no longer liked him. I let go of hurt, rejection, resentment, and abandonment. I found ME!

There is a way out of addiction and depression. But not without the work, time, effort, and goals. You can unpack your depression and stay stuck in the past, or you can find a new passion. Over the past decade, I learned much about depression, manic behavior, addiction, and narcissism. You cannot make someone snap out of or suck up their depression in that deep phase. The true antidote to loneliness is connection. Do not wait for your friends to come to you, do a mental check every day if you must. It could mean a difference in their life. ***"don't ask why the addiction, ask why the trauma"****- Gabor Mate.* Depression is the same. What is the trauma behind the depression?

Some people say that you will not leave someone you love if they have cancer, as it is not their choice to be sick. Therefore, mental health issues are the same. It is not their choice to be in that place of feeling depressed. It may be an unpopular opinion, but their choice is to seek help and get out of their hopeless state. You have the power to choose your therapy and overcome your past regrets and traumas. Use those experiences as lessons, nothing is constant, and change only happens when you take control of your own life. I do not believe you should give up your own life if someone you love has mental health issues and they choose not to seek help. Your mental health is just as important as theirs. Do not stay in any relationship that harms your own mental health. *Jim Rohn quote,* ***"you take care of you for me, and I will take care of me for you."*** We all need to do our part to care for our mental health. That is your responsibility.

If you want to break the stigma of mental health, do not wait for someone to ask for help, be a friend and do a friend check. Your door may always be open, but theirs is always closed. Be willing to sit in the uncomfortable silence and be available to listen to the stories and the uncertainty in mind.

The stigma is changing, and men are more accepting of showing emotions and discussing their vulnerabilities. The suicide rate for men is higher than that of women, but women have more attempted suicides. Men have a higher risk of turning to alcohol and substance abuse with their mental health issues as a way of masking their issues.

Men struggle with trying to be strong in the times they feel weak. It is only when they feel safe, that they will show vulnerability. Everyone has emotions and they learn both acceptable and unjustifiable ways to deal with them. These are their coping mechanisms for survival. We are learning to let men show emotions. Unfortunately, we want them to still be strong all the time. They struggle to be both strong and vulnerable. It is hard for them to be both, having grown up believing that showing emotions makes you weak. To have both strength and emotions is to be human.

The Man behind the mask

WHO IS HE, *the man I see?*

The man behind the mask.

He hides behind his mask of shame from all his childhood pain.

He provides for his family with all he has and would die to save their life.

He buries his pain and heartache for all the friends and loves he lost.

He knows he cannot protect and save them all but does his best to try.

He cannot describe the love he feels and how it aches inside.

He buries his guilt and his vulnerability to not feel "less than a man."

Be a man – that does not cry and does not show emotions.

Be a man – carry the weight and protect all that is yours.

Be a man – stand up tall and never back down from anything.

It must be hard to be a man.

It must be difficult to wear the mask.

It must be lonely to never freely express your emotions.

It must be tough to be strong despite the times you feel weak.

Love is not Enough

As time goes by, we realize that love is not enough to hold on to our partners. We need more in our life to make all relationships work. Not just with partners but with our children and our parents. Love is Not Enough. You can love someone with everything in you. You can feel like they were your everything. You can have great memories. They could be your greatest lessons. But one day you learn the Love is not enough. You need communication. You need goals and values aligned. You need trust and honesty. You need to know they got your back in everything. You need commitment and reliability. You need compassion and acceptance. You need commonality and passion. Love alone is never enough to get you through the good and bad days.

The older I get in my life, I realize that as much as I wanted my love for someone to be enough to make them want to try to be better or do better, this was never the case. It is hard because that is where our lack of worthiness stems from. We attach our worthiness to someone else's love for us. How reliable they are to us, what they are willing to do, give up or change. Our worthiness of being or feeling love is based on the power of someone else's ability to love us the way we desire and need. Our worthiness should stem from our internal source, not our external forces. We should never give someone that much power to make us enough. We are ENOUGH without anyone, and we should never settle for less than we deserve. The problem is most people have never had role models for teaching them those standards or values in their life. So, any love is good love.

We want our children or parents to know we love them, yet we fail to tell them, show them, or spend time with them. As much as we want people in our life to just know how much we love them, they do not always realize it. We all speak different love languages to meet our need for love and connection. We need to look for the signs of their love because it is not always the words "I love you." Some people have a tough time expressing their love feelings. My daughter says, "I love you", when she pats the top of my head. Since she was a teenager, she was not much for saying I love you or giving me hugs. But she had little gestures that told me otherwise. She still loved me. I take them and realize she is still learning her place in her journey and think I will be here forever. My son has always shown more affection towards me, and the older he got, the easier it came. He had realized a lot about life and love through experiences and loss. He finally admitted I was a good mom, and I did the best I could. His love gestures are his big squishy hugs, telling me I love you, and lots of small gestures. But it has all been a work in progress along the way.

We tend to pull away from our parents at a certain point in our life, knowing our journey does not involve them or their advice. It is our life to live, our experiences, and our mistakes to make. Eventually, we come back to them, seeking their knowledge and experience. Usually, this happens when we become parents ourselves. Then, we realized parenting was much tougher than we gave them credit for. There was much more to it than just the words I love you. But love came in many different forms in the way they taught us and gave up their time for us so we could have a better life than the generations before us.

Every relationship has a learning curve. Our values and beliefs change over time. Our needs are different at various stages of our life. Sometimes we rely on love to get us through the tough days, remembering at one-time love was enough to get us through. Love meant something. We all reach a point that love is not enough for a sustainable relationship. People think relationships must be hard, but they are not. They just need constant communication as you shift through transitions and chapters of your life. Every relationship you have creates a shift in your needs, wants and sometimes your goals. Your priorities and your identity shift. You need to learn to flow with each other and communicate.

Everyone wants a happy life and thinks that holding on to a love that once was great at some point is the answer. But everything has an expiration date. You must recognize that a relationship or friendship has run its course and let it go. It is loving to do this for both of you. You can both move on to a happier and more fulfilling life and future by yourself or with someone else. It is the kindest thing to do for each of you. Sometimes we hold on too long because we imagine someone else getting the best part of that person. Remember, you had the best part of that person at the beginning of the relationship. Each person gives us new lessons so we can hopefully be better in the next relationship. Holding on too long just prolongs both of you from finding happiness and love again. True love is letting go so the other person can be happy. Loving yourself is letting go of the people that no longer give you peace, joy, love, and happiness.

Soulmates

Soulmates are not always the person that is meant to be in your life forever but the one that changes you forever. A soulmate may be the love of your life that your heart longs for to make it whole. A soulmate may bring you to your authentic self. A soulmate will accept you for who you are exactly as you are, with all your imperfections. A soulmate may come in and out of your life a few times until the universe aligns all the connections to make it last. It is possible to have more than just one soulmate.

You will know your true love soulmate when you meet them. Something inside just feels intense. There is a feeling of protection and love that is so indescribable. You cannot imagine your world without them and go to the ends of the earth just to be by their side forever.

The legend is that two people who are meant to be together have a red string of love attached to both their ankles, and they will consistently find their way back without hesitation of connection. The string may stretch and tangle but never break.

I thought I had found this in one person, but that connection was only to take each of us to a better version of ourselves. At least, for me, it was! When you do not learn the lessons in a relationship, you will easily fall back into the same patterns of love and life. It may not be the same person, but the lessons will repeat.

My true love soulmate, whom I found 30 years ago, yet not really understanding that we would be together several times throughout our life as we had drifted in and out of each other's lives temporarily. I knew the intensity of the deep emotions that surrounded us each time. Sometimes we overlook the greatest love in front of us until it is too late. I realized the depth of the longing for this person when we shared an intense unexplainable connection. I know we had to go our separate ways to live out the chapters in our life, to bring us to the best chapter of our life together. We had to go through the same experiences differently to fully appreciate and love from the depths of our souls together. My experiences have allowed me to love both him and me unconditionally, without limitations and judgement. Without insecurities and without ego. I accept loving myself and, therefore, can love someone without these same conditions or expectations. Just pure true love. I always knew in my heart this was the man I was meant to marry. Now, it has become our reality. I look forward to the journey together with him.

Love takes you on a journey that you may never understand. It has so many lessons. Years ago, I found the man I recently married. I knew it from all our shared times together. I even wrote in my journal 28 years ago that he was the man I would marry. We dated and lived together briefly. Our love was strong, but life had a different plan that would take us apart for several years. We each married and divorced, had children, and raised stepchildren. He found me years ago, but the universe was not ready to align us forever yet. Time passed, and we kept each other in our hearts but just let it be.

He had to leave to be a father to his only son. It was an ultimatum he was given. He made the right decision but realized communication may have helped us to get through it together. I married his cousin and had my own children. After ten years, I separated from my husband, and we reconnected briefly. We discussed a relationship, but because he and his cousin never got along, it seemed like more hassles than it was worth. We vaguely stayed connected through the years, leading separate lives. Following my last separation, he unexpectedly invited me for coffee (twelve years later.)

Neither of us was searching for a relationship, yet here we are, making a future together. He took me on a motorcycle ride that cemented us like magic. He took my hand and put it in his pocket to keep warm. I had instant tears in my eyes. When I was a little girl riding a snowmobile, my dad did the same thing. I always felt protected and loved. This was the moment I knew; he was the one!

Our relationship quickly took shape, forming the best bond either of us has ever had. I knew I had forever found my love, partner, and best friend. We have both lived so much life and have grown into the best version of ourselves. We are happy with our life. We knew we were always supposed to marry each other. It was all about timing. For him, I was the one that got away. I am glad he never gave up. This is where I am meant to be. With him is my happy place!

The story's twist is that my children have his last name because it was the same as his cousins. I kept my given name throughout my marriage. Life has an ironic way of working out.

Sometimes you can achieve more in a few months with the right person than you did in a lifetime with someone else. You have more communication, balance, and understanding together. Everything just aligns with the perfect connection. You realize neither of you is perfect, but you do not dwell on flaws because that person is perfect for you. They love you, respect you and protect you better than anyone has. Love and energy just flow. You work well together because you both know your roles. True love creates no demands, and no ego is present. There is a balance of values and goals in life.

Knowing you are heading in the same direction, it is easier with one another for support. Someone to trust and rely on. The relationship has both passion and peace.

A true love soulmate will always find their way to you. They may come in and out of your life until everything aligns, and it is your time to truly be in balance and harmony. Understanding that everything you went through was to bring you to a place of acceptance moving forward. You put in your time and lessons with other people and relationships so you can fully cherish and love one another. Love is about the acceptance of flaws without change. Being generous with one another while maintaining your boundaries. Learning to communicate and not attack in judgement. Learning to listen to understand instead of reacting or responding. If you find your true love soulmate, take the time to feel the beauty in the heart and touch. True love is not hard work, just working together for the same goals.

Communication is truly the key to a successful partnership. You build a foundation of trust, integrity, and love by having tough conversations. We fall in love easily but staying in love takes compromise and a willingness to commit through the good and tough times. With true love, you know in your heart that this person is your protector, supporter, and best friend.

Now is the time to be open-minded and to just allow the flow of energies to be one. Explore all emotions and new communication. Never take a connection like this for granted. It only comes around once in your lifetime. If you blink, you may miss the opportunity in front of you.

If you are lucky enough to find your soulmate and fall in love, treasure the connection.

Two voices

I HEAR two voices inside my head, one that pushes me to the edge, the other holds me closer. There is one that tells me life is too hard. It is the one that says, "just give up because you will never be good enough." My inner critic pushes me away from people, places and opportunities and have the life I want to live. It is the fear inside that holds me back. The voice that pushes me to the edge says, "Hold on tight, this is as good as it gets. You are too fat, you are too skinny, you will never be pretty enough." This is the voice that compares us to other people's life. It is the voice that has judgement of others as much as you judge yourself. It takes over your emotions and thoughts and keeps you stuck in patterns. This voice judges and does not listen to what my emotions are. It is the voice that blames, creates shame and guilt for all the wrong choices I have made. It is the voice inside I can hear, but it always makes me think twice. There must be a better way.

The other voice I hear inside is the one that holds me close. The soothing voice that speaks to me. The one that says it loves me unconditionally. Despite all my wrongs, I did okay. I made the choices that were right that day. I can do anything that comes from the purest intention of love. It creates validation and understanding that *I will always be enough*. It is the voice of *self-love* and uses fear as good. It will push you to the limits of learning, so you can try new things. It is a voice of empathy and reason, the one that says, "I will catch you when you fall." The inner voice that makes me believe; it understands my need to be loved. That I deserve all the best and can reach any goal I set. This Journey is mine, and I am never alone. Just learn to live for today. The voice that holds me close tells me, "My pain is just temporary. You will always find a way through. You are built to endure with strength and love. You are courageous and brave!"

The inner critic is your survival mode and holds on to the past. It keeps you stuck in comfort, fearful of enjoying life. The soothing voice is pure and loving. It pulls you in when life is tough but propels you towards greater things. Listen to the voice that holds you close and teaches you how to love. It teaches you that life has lessons to learn and share. Keep moving forward.

When we realize we can choose which voice we listen to, we have more power to shut the other down. We sometimes get sucked into listening to our inner critic, the one that never takes the stage. But we can learn we have control and can diminish those voices that keep our patterns stuck in a hamster's cage. This takes digging deep into the inner work and discovering what is real. We learn we can recover from all that we feel blame, shame, and guilt for.

Learning to love yourself and realize your own worth is the greatest gift you will give yourself every day. Learning you always have a choice which voice you listen to daily is a great part of recovering what you can control.

Self – Love deficit

I WOULD NEVER HAVE CONSIDERED myself to have a self-love deficit. I grew up only having a few friends, more like acquaintances, but we spent time together just the same. Both my parents were loving, and I never doubted their love at any point in my life. My parents separated when I was young, and my brother grew up with my dad. My mother was sick through the years, and I took care of her. I was fearful for years of her dying and leaving me. I never realized my fear of abandonment until recently, when I also concluded that I had interpreted it into a fear of rejection. I had projected this from many relationships that did not work out and created a self-rejection.

I endured my fair share of heartbreaking relationships, a few made choices that were best for them at that moment. But this left me in a state of feeling rejected and lost for a period. I was also mentally strong, motivated, determined, and independent. To the point of extreme independence as a self-preservation survival mode. This I know can also be trauma-based. I did not have much of a childhood and had to learn a lot of tasks at an early age, as there was no "man of the house," and my mother did not have a clue of how to do certain things. I was determined to learn. To this day I still do many things independently. I find it empowering to be independent. I have also taught the same to my children, yet they know I have their back when needed. Just like my family had mine.

In my first marriage, I had boundaries, self-love, self-respect, and self-worth. My children were young, and they were my priority. After that, something changed. As a mother raising two kids and having no friends, I traded my loneliness for what I thought was lasting happiness. My second-long term relationship became my addiction to codependency. It started so great, our connection was instant, and escalation happened quickly. I am unsure when it all shifted as it had many good and bad moments. But as time went on, the alcohol addiction in my partner became increasingly noticeable, and my loneliness returned. I started to sacrifice my happiness and that of my children for crumbs of meeting my needs of love and connection. The relationship became my addiction. I tried to control it more and ended up with less. I wanted to save them all but could not save myself or them. I wanted my happiness back yet became increasingly more resentful.

As I started my journey of knowledge and acceptance of the understanding of relationships and myself, I discovered that I had a lot to figure out. I realized there was a lot I needed to take ownership of in my life and my relationships with others. I realized I had lacked some self-love, respect, and, most of all, boundaries.

As I regained consciousness and understood the chaos and dysfunction of my relationship and family life, I knew something had to change. I became aware of my new path but had to figure out how to implement and follow through. If there were changes to be made, someone would not be happy. I started shifting my own life and decisions and taking back my power. I started to stand up for myself and not back down. I opened my eyes to what I was feeling and what I was allowing to happen. As often as I was told about the situation, I chose to dismiss it and not believe it. I didn't do enough to change the situation. I was in denial of how bad it was or how simple it was to leave the situation. I always felt it would be better after we talked about it. Next time it would be different. It would not happen again. It was a lack of communication, boundaries, values and eventually broken hearts.

Whenever he turned to alcohol, marijuana, other friends, or hobbies, it took away from us. I felt like I was the last choice of convenience. We just drifted away from priorities and our life together. We both became lonely and turned to different distractions in life. The more boundaries and self-respect I created, the more resistance I got from him. I was not backing down this time. I was taking my life back!

It was my partner that was lost in a self-love deficit and narcissistic traits. He did not love himself, could not be alone, and had traits of a narcissist of not caring about others' needs over his own needs. He came first, no matter what. He never felt good enough or loved enough as a child, having grown up in an alcoholic dysfunctional family without learning how to cope and survive in his world. He became distracted by alcohol, drugs, and self-glorification and gratification. He wore a mask for many years until it was too much to handle. His lifelong charade had ended, and he could no longer play the part.

The stronger I became in owning my mistakes and realizing the new direction of my life with self-love and boundaries, the more he pulled away due to his unwillingness to change or grow. His true colors really started to glow. His mental illness created a person I no longer loved or respected. This was the alter ego that played the most puzzling mind games and made me feel rejected, unloved, and crazy. I kept repeating to myself how rejected I felt in many of the moments of despair.

I went through loneliness, heartbreak, and self-rejection to the point of starting to crash and feeling mentally drained. As soon as I understood it was up to me to pull myself out, everything shifted with the knowledge I already had inside me. At the darkest moments, I decided I was taking back my life. I was going to live each day with passion, adventure, and gratitude. I owned the fact that it was me keeping myself stuck in the pattern of rejection. A wave of instant power took over, and I became focused on my self-worth, self-respect, boundaries, and most of all, self-love.

I became my own best friend, and my life started to become more fulfilled than I ever remembered in my entire life.

We will all have moments of loneliness, boredom, and challenges of emotions. Get curious about them. Where did they stem from? What are they trying to teach you? They are only a symptom, not a cause of your inner voice. Do not be numb with distractions of life or the need to constantly be filling a void. Get clarity on your life and your goals, and live with gratitude. Your life will change.

Forgiveness

Forgiving someone is a choice, but you need to do it for yourself. Living with anger, frustration and hurt only harms yourself and no one else. When someone hurts you, let it go. Not for them but for your own mental health. There are so many factors of emotional pain. People are driven by emotions. Are you driven by fear, hate or love? Sometimes we struggle with forgiveness, as the emotional pain has gone on for too long, and we do not see perspective. We continue to be stuck in a spot where forgiveness does not seem possible. Shift perspective and realize those moments of hurt have given you something greater. A sense of yourself. When you feel anger, a sense of betrayal or unjustified, you will push yourself to new limits. It is an opportunity to get involved in a cause, evolve within us, or shift perspectives. Some people have difficulty looking for the positives. They get stuck in the hurt and anger emotions for too long. This only leads to blame and resentment.

Look at the situation, learn the lessons and move on. Always apologize for your own wrongdoing and take ownership " it is better to be happy than it is to be right". Most people will forgive if the situation has been acknowledged. I forgive because I learned the lesson. I realized that all the emotional pain I endured made me stronger. It has led me on a journey I may not have taken. We make all decisions based on the things we know now. Feel the love and forgive yourself. It will make you a better person as you are not competing with anyone. You can be a better person today than you were yesterday.

Certain circumstances and unforgivable situations that do not deserve forgiveness are our biggest why's. Why did this happen? So, when you can find the lesson or the courage to help someone else through something just as terrible and unforgiving, this is your why. It will never change the situation, but it changes the outcome of your healing. You do not need to give forgiveness or let it go. But take the pain as an opportunity for helping to heal others and become one with your power and strength to survive the pain.

Forgiveness is a big part of acceptance, healing and letting go. If you cannot forgive, you allow past circumstances to steal your power and hold you in its clutches of anger and fear. When you do not let go and make amends with the past, you do not allow yourself to fully love, trust or live to the extent of enjoying life. Accept the event for what it was, a place in time. Trauma is created by the meaning you give to the moment and the emotions you feel. It may be valid, but it will keep you stuck long after the situation occurs. Forgiving someone for causing you pain is difficult and feels unjustified, but you are the only one holding on to pain. Time to release it and not give it energy and allow them to still win in creating ongoing trauma. Take back your life and take back your power. You are the warrior now.

Sometimes we hold on to the anger others caused us instead of the lesson. We need to ask ourselves, if plans had worked out differently, would I have still taken the path I did? Chances are NO. We are taken to places of struggle to become a different person than we believed. When possible, shift your perspective to not be angry that someone did you wrong. Instead, thank them for showing you the person you could be. Thank them for having more courage to walk away and for the strength you created for yourself.

Before we can truly forgive, we must also learn what it means to apologize to ourselves and others. Apologies are important as a way of connecting to the validation and emotions of the other person; it is about taking ownership that you did something wrong. It allows for empathy but does not guarantee forgiveness. Apologizing is exceedingly difficult if you were never taught how to do it as a child. I struggled with apologizing, and it is the one thing I am working hard at doing right instead of being right. Sometimes we do not realize when we hurt each other or have overstepped our boundaries. Therefore, we go into defensiveness trying to state our case versus apologizing and forgiving. We do not communicate properly. We are all a work in progress with something that helps us grow and improve ourselves and our relationships. Just when you think you got it, someone will test you, showing you there is always more work to do.

Stop over apologizing! You can apologize for situations you may have caused and take ownership but stop over apologizing. It will keep you in a shame spiral, and it will not change a thing. You know from your own emotions that you will not simply forgive an apology until you are ready to let it go and forgive the person you feel created your pain. Unfortunately, people will use this manipulation to keep you in a guilt cycle by controlling your power of forgiveness. It allows someone else to determine your worthiness and self-confidence. Release it and allow the other person to have their emotions and deal with them on their own time frame of healing.

GET honest about loving yourself unconditionally. Learning to love yourself is the hardest love we can give. Most of us think we love ourselves, therefore, if we think it, so it must be true. But what does it mean genuinely love yourself? Stop and think about it. Think of everything you have done for yourself daily and throughout your life without anyone else's influence. Was it for you, or was there a hidden agenda for someone else? Being honest with yourself means you must know your true values, beliefs, wants and needs. That would be a good start when you understand all those things and can live within your boundaries. Love yourself positively, and live your life loving each day and everything about you. If you want to change, make it in a positive direction that brings you closer to your dreams and goals. Remembering life is all about you. Remember, do not intentionally harm anyone along the way.... live your life unstoppably. Love a passion and live for it.

People that constantly live with depression, loneliness, blame, resentment, and body pain manifestation. They have not learned to love themselves unconditionally. They have not allowed themselves time to find purpose, direction, and passion. They do not know how to rewrite their story and start again. They have not learned they are in control of their own lives and destination. It is time for those people to ask themselves... why am I not happy? What would make me happy? Most of all... what am I going to do about it?

The blame or resentment we feel for others is usually a blame or resentment we have created based on our actions, reactions, thoughts, and feelings. Most times, the blame, envy and resentment are truly about us for not choosing a different path, for not standing up for ourselves and allowing others to make our decisions, and for allowing others to take control. In other words, we were not authentic to ourselves. Think of a situation, now or in the future, when you are blaming someone else.... think of your expectations and why you are really blaming them. Most times we create blame as we do not know how to take ownership and accountability. We do not realize that others do not always know what we feel or think. For example, if you expect others in your household to offer to help and they do not... you blame them for their inconsiderate behavior and resent them for never offering. If you never asked for what you wanted, you cannot expect them to know you need help. Just appreciate the moments they do or ask for help. But do not resent them in the moments you expect them to read your mind. Set a standard of what you want and expect from day 1, so everyone is on the same page of expectation. Most times we believe that how we see the world is how everyone sees the world. We do not realize everyone has different expectations, different viewpoints, and different under-standing. We expect others to react just as we would. If that were possible, there would be no growth in learning or life experiences. Always be open to seeing a point from another perspective. It does not mean you have to agree, but always be willing to listen, ask questions and learn.

There can be difficulties in any relationship. Most times we are unsure how to handle these issues. We feel like someone is blaming us for their feelings. At times we all have feelings of resentment, blame and useless suffering. We blame others for controlling us, yet we forget about situations we allowed to happen or created. When we allow others to take over when we should be responsible, we become resentful when we want our control back. Usually, this happens when we just hope things will change, yet we lack proper communication skills and openness. We forget that our needs are different from our partners. We assume they are the same. We forget how we see things is not how someone else sees them. It becomes a lack of understanding on both ends. When this situation continues for an extended period, we become unsure if there is hope in sight for a change. Is it possible to change the way we perceive things? To learn to understand that; it is all about how I am receiving it and not really how the situation is? Open communication is key in changing anything in life. Anything worth changing is going to be a challenge.

Learning to accept people for who they are can be a challenge. When we struggle to accept someone wholeheartedly, we must understand that it is our thoughts and feelings that we are truly rejecting. To accept our own thoughts and feelings means we must be real with ourselves. To understand that part in someone may reflect a part of our past we have rejected for some reason. When we try to change someone to suit our needs, we may think it will make us happy, but it may change everything we know about the other person. If people were not happy with themselves, wouldn't they change? Sometimes people do not know how to or have just accepted their life as the way it is. People do not always realize life can be better or different. Acceptance and trust make people happy.

An example is someone who is a smoker or a drinker; it is better for their health not to do these things. But asking them to change to suit your needs is setting a restriction on love. If they choose to change those things, they will. Until that person decides to change, accept them just the way they are. If their behavior is a problem, so is your acceptance. This is a difference in values. If they are happy, most times, it is our acceptance that is a problem, not the issue at hand. You do not have to accept someone else's behavior just because that is them. Acceptance does not mean you have to like them. Sometimes what makes others happy does not fit into your life. You accept what you need and want. After all, life is also about your happiness also. When you cannot accept the behavior of others, and it affects your life, it is time to move on. Happiness in any relationship is two-sided. Both people must be happy for true love to exist. No relationship should ever be one-sided. It is not always going to be equal; life is never 50/50. Love with everything you have and accept all that is given.

As much as we want to feel happy all the time in our lives and our relationships, this creates a huge demand for ourselves and others. We need to have the downs so we can appreciate the ups. We need the good times to experience the difference in the struggles. To understand the suffering so we can be grateful for the love. In every relationship, from partners and children to parents, there will always be moments when it is easier to run than to face the situations at hand. What does running accomplish? Are you willing to throw everything away to be without the challenge of true love? Being on your own does not guarantee happiness. Only you can create change. Only by suffering does it motivate us to make a change in any aspect of our life. When we are in a comfortable state, we do not change or grow. As the saying goes, "you are either living or dying," but only you choose.

Sometimes we struggle between doing good because it just feels right and the "what about me" feelings. When we give so much to everyone else, we forget about giving to the one person that matters most in our life. ME! I have had a personal struggle with this for many years, with caring and giving to others, making them feel loved, appreciated, accepted, trusting, and supported by others. I have given a lot of myself over the years, yet have sometimes become disassociated, hurt, and resentful. I have given so much and felt so little in return. Expecting someone else to do for me what I do for them is a feeling of respect. I learned that these are my expectations only, and it is not about respect. Forgetting everyone is different. I do what I do for others because it makes me happy. Sometimes we become codependent. We enable others as a way of over helping and taking away their ability to grow and have natural consequences. We become addicted to helping, nurturing, and controlling, believing that without us, their life would be different, and so would ours. We create a fulfillment of self in helping others. Unfortunately, this also creates resentment towards us and others. We need to learn a balance in taking care of ME.... and the ones we love. It is not up to anyone else to take care of us or create our happiness, but sometimes we do need help, guidance, and support along the way. No matter what... we all need to feel loved, supported and appreciated. Ultimately remembering, I am in charge of creating my own happiness. It is my responsibility to be HAPPY.

Looking back through life, we realize the past explains a lot of our present and learning to let it go is difficult. It is easier to blame than to take responsibility for every choice, every action, and every reaction in our life. We have many struggles that are relevant to our life. Understanding that everyone has had challenges to face and each person's obstacles are relevant to their life, just as yours is to you. The biggest challenge is not allowing your past to define your present or future. Not realizing how our past affects our present life is difficult. We can only change what we are aware of if we choose to change.

We tend to think "what ifs" and look back to the past to see what we could have done differently to change the situation. We have all been the bad parent and felt we could have done more in any given circumstance. We all feel we never give enough knowledge, time, understanding or love. At the time we are giving all we know and have. As my mother taught me...." *you can only make decisions with the knowledge and feelings you have at that time. If you made the wrong choice, you could make a change.*" Good advice sometimes seems so hard to live by. Like many other people, I would have made different choices *if* I could do it all over. Now I am trying to figure out the best path for ME. As a responsible parent, my children are the focus of my life. Somehow, I lost that focus and am trying to rebuild it. We all get lost or distracted from time to time on our own path. Back on track now and still learning lessons along the way.

Every now and again we need to step back and re-evaluate the person that matters most, "ME." As much as we want to make everyone around us happy, we cannot. The only person that truly needs to be Happy is ME. When I am happy, so is everyone around me. When your cup overflows, it overflows to others, and they want to be around you. Whatever your cup is full of that is what others feel through the ripple effect. So how do we do you get happy? Good question.... first realize *you* are the most important person in your life. Your wants and needs matter. Take some time to get away from everyone you usually hang around with or live with. We all need a break so we can appreciate others just as they can appreciate us. Taking a break is a wonderful way to realize the importance of what you want and need in your life. Try things you have not done before to realize your potential.

We never give ourselves credit as sometimes we try to play the part of the stories we think we should fit into. Most times the person we become as a spouse or a parent, even a friend, is not the *me* I want to be, and we forget how to be the person we were inside. Let loose, let go and just be in the moment. Forget the responsibilities of life and just HAVE FUN. Find a balance, there is a time to forget responsibilities, and there is a time to take ownership and responsibility for family, love, and life. There is a time for self-care and a time for the people you love. There is time for all of it!

In any relationship there will be struggles as it challenges us to see things from someone else's perspective. We will never agree 100% with everyone in our life. It strengthens our beliefs and ethics, allows us to be strong in the way we see life, or challenges the growth of our minds and different perspectives. Sometimes in these moments we must remember that one person's opinion does not mean that we are wrong; people are simply different. We are all raised and matured differently and need to accept what is true as different. Never accept that people are just going to believe you. It just does not happen that way. Could you imagine a world where everyone agreed? Everyone had the same belief systems, same ethics and no one challenged one another. There would be no growth. So, remember the next time you become frustrated with someone's opinion that they are challenging your way of thinking or their own. Through discussions we learn to see the world through someone else's perspective of life, which in fact, can be a rewarding experience if you let it. Most people do not see it that way. Too many of us take life too personally. Someone else's thoughts or perception is only a reflection of all their life and thoughts. Love someone for who they are, not whom you wish them to be.

"All those that wander are not lost", and sometimes we are lost for a while, but that is only so we can know the difference between what we think we want and what we genuinely want. Sometimes we get so caught up in living in the moment of someone else's life and dreams that we lose sight of our dreams and goals. Sometimes we do not know our purpose, goals, or dreams as we are so busy giving attention to our parents, partners, and children. We do not realize we can choose to live our own lives, seek paths, and follow our passion.

A shift happens when we realize I am the only one that can truly make me happy, and I am responsible for making me happy. I understand that I create my own rules and follow my own boundaries and ethics. I am in control of how I allow others to treat me and make me feel. I became HAPPY when I realized what I wanted and how I wanted to live. I chose my destiny and the path I travel. I decided that if others wanted to be a part of my life, it was their choice just as much as it was mine. I decided to put my boundaries back in place and follow my heart. Everyone has a choice in life as to which path they want to take, and sometimes we only travel together for a while and sometimes forever. When we shift in our life, shifts happen in those around us. Sometimes for the positive and some become the lessons. Life is never constant. Life is shifting, growing, and constantly changing.

Sometimes we become an enabler in a relationship. As a parent, we enable our children from becoming who they need to be. It is easier to help them find their way than allow the struggle. You only grow and learn when you struggle. In a love relationship, we can get caught up in loving and doing so much for someone else that each person forgets that Love and relationships are a partnership. Although you each give 100% into a relationship, both share the 100/100 rule... as love is giving and taking. You respect and treat the other person the way you want. We tend to feel overwhelmed with gratitude in the beginning that we allow it to happen. Suddenly, everything changes as one person continues to take on that role. Instead, we need to learn to switch roles of the giver and the receiver. We give 100% effort as we know we have ups and downs and sometimes rely on the other person to make the difference. For constant growth people need to take ownership and responsibility for each action. It may feel easier to take over, but resentment can grow quickly. When you expect that things will just change without constant communication and comprehension, it becomes a lack of awareness. Both people stop trying and start blaming. The ego takes over, and it becomes everyone else's fault.

So many possibilities open when you are in the space of self-love. You do not care about the opinions of others or what they think of you. You create a world of self-care and self-respect. You know your values and can set boundaries without guilt, moving forward and without shame from the past. You let go of who you thought you should be and become the person you are meant to be.

Self- Love is about letting go of the world around you and falling in love with yourself. It is the acceptance that you are amazing just as you are. You were never meant to be perfect, but always a work in progress. Self-love is about understanding your worth and not negotiating that value with anyone else.

SELF-LOVE LESSONS

- *I learned to let go of the people that no longer deserve to be in my life; they were no longer good to me or appreciated my time and energy.*
- *I learned that I do not NEED anyone to make me HAPPY and that I can be happy on my own and in my own space.*
- *I learned that respect for myself was of greater importance than respect for someone that did not reciprocate.*
- *I learned that it is not my job to please or make others happy, but we can share our happiness together.*
- *I learned that my self-care is important and may look and feel different from yours.*
- *I learned that I could fill up my own cup of happiness without filling a void or creating a distraction from my thoughts and feelings.*
- *I learned that you could have happy, healthy relationships and still honor yourself without giving up your values.*
- *I learned that I could be authentic with self-love, and the right people will love me for who I am, not what I can give them.*

When you learn self-love, you are willing to walk away from anything that is not made for you anymore. A willingness to stand tall, believe in yourself and keep pushing forward despite anything the critics tell you.

Love yourself without ego, feel the passion in your heart to be alive and walk through life confidently. Live each day with gratitude. Today is the first day of the rest of your life, but tomorrow could be your last. Choose wisely the life you want to live.

Untamed

We all have a little piece inside that is wild and untamed. It is the part of us we bury, or only a few may see. For others, the wild one took over many years of their life. Being untamed is about letting go and showing the world your beauty in all its glory. The ability to show up and unleash whatever is right now in the moment. We all have pieces of our identity that we allow others to see daily, the parts we think others will accept. Let them start to accept all of you. When you can start showing up exactly as you are, you have found your tribe. A sense of acceptance is released when you find the person that allows your wild one inside to be free from judgement and accepts the part of your soul you buried to be alive.

When you get the chance, do not be afraid to let the untamed out to play for a while. Let go of the inhibitions that chain you. Your soul needs a reprieve.

Being untamed is about allowing yourself to be vulnerable and authentic at the same time. We want to learn to live life passionately, have adventures, and live our goals and dreams. Achieving proud moments and loving life on our terms.

Most of our life we need to be responsible, respectable and in control of our decisions and the consequences of our choice. We rarely get to be free to be spontaneous and courageous, to follow our heart to do whatever we need to, just to satisfy the wild one inside.

The untamed or wild one is the inner child that has to learn to be responsible as both the child and then the adult. Our inner child comes in many forms. Overall, a child needs to have structure, play and connection. Sometimes the inner child was pushed down for being too loud, too outspoken, and just wanting their own freedom. The inner child wanted no responsibilities for anyone and no worries about adult life. Even in adulthood our inner child needs to play. Through our 20s and 50s we have more of an untamed or true self that we permit to set free. We have no kids and are free to explore the world's wonders. In our 20s, we are rushing, trying to experience freedom from parents, education for our future, traveling and living a social life before we settle down with kids. After 45 years of age and the children leave home on their own journeys, we realize there were so many dreams and goals we wanted to accomplish yet did not. We can now afford to start living life on our terms, and we become a little more untamed as we start to date again, go on adventures or just rediscover who we are for the first time after having kids.

Our identity was engulfed by raising children for the past 20 years. We are unsure of who we are or what we like. We will always be the mom, the parent, the greatest supporter, and the biggest fan of our children. Our decisions for our own success and happiness have nothing to do with them or the outcome it will play on them. It is all on us. We can be spontaneous and free; we do not have to check in or be responsible for anyone but ourselves. It is AWESOME!

Life becomes uniquely different for some. My long-term relationship ended, so I no longer felt bound to the responsibilities of being a stepparent. My roles shifted with all the children. My son had been living on his own, trying out ideas of entrepreneurship and college for a few years. He was discovering his own path in life. Now it is time for my daughter to spread her wings and fly. Although the trajectory of both of their life's changed due to lockdowns and shutdowns with Covid, they are both in the untamed stage of their own life. A chance to discover new people, unfamiliar places, and new experiences. A time to discover their identity and live life on their terms.

If we learned to live life a little more untamed, we would not always be searching for a sense of belonging.

Happy begins with me

I AM at a point in my life I am happy. Happy begins with me, and I can share it with those around me. I never needed a lot of friends but appreciated the ones I had. I like my own company and can amuse myself for hours unless I procrastinate on what needs to be done and do not want to do it. Common in most people. I love looking at perspectives and learning from others by people watching. I learned a lot about myself by what I like or do not like, what I judge or overlook, and my opinions or other people's choices or values. Sometimes we learn what we like by understanding what we do not like.

I still get sucked into past triggers that I keep working on through *"the story I tell myself"* (a lesson from Brene Brown). I am sure this will often happen as I deal with each trigger from past relationships or self-thoughts, doubts, and emotions. Healing is a process of digging deep with acknowledgement and understanding of self and other people. When we get sucked into self-pity, we need to remind ourselves to take nothing other people do personally. They have a reason or plan. Sometimes we think an emotional attack is personal, but other people have stress building up in their life that they do not know how to handle. People have values that they choose over other people's lifestyles or want. That is part of guilt-free living. When my happiness begins with me, I am making the choices I need in my life. I am learning to honor my needs and wants without the expense of others.

For many years I lacked trust in others and had to work through the triggers of whether it was the person, the pattern, or my internal dialogue that kept me stuck in distrust. Most often it was all the above. The trust issue may have had different underlying reasons, but the patterns were the same. I had to learn to trust my instincts and yet take ownership for the times I allowed old hurts to invade my new relationships. It is not that we are afraid of new love, just afraid of old pain. So, we justify or seek red flags before they happen.

One lesson I wish I would have learned earlier in life was, "Never stay somewhere you are unhappy." The older we get, the more we realize we do not need anyone's permission to leave. We can make the decisions that make us happy and are not responsible for others' happiness. Unfortunately, we get stuck in situations where we feel obligated to stick it out and make it work because we have committed to someone or something. That is why people stay in jobs or relationships too long. Fear of upsetting others, yet you continue hurting yourself by staying too long. This only builds resentment and disrespect. Your happiness is not negotiable with anyone, yet we feel guilty for wanting to break a commitment. No more- you come first! Your happiness comes first. This is not selfish. This is self-care! Your mental health is just as important as the person holding you back from living and loving life. You can get a new job, new friends, and new relationships, but there is only one you. This is the biggest lesson I would like to teach my children. It would save a lot of heartaches and wasted time on people or jobs that take away years of a happy life. I no longer feel guilty for walking away from the people or things in my life if it takes away from my happiness. From now on, I choose to live life happy!

We all want to belong or fit in somewhere, but unfortunately, it comes at the expense of our own authenticity. If we are unsure of who we are and what our values are, we will struggle even more and lose ourselves trying to be like everyone else. Fitting in is adjusting and adapting to those around us, so we can create a connection beyond ourselves. True belonging just feels right, with no adjustments or adaptations to change yourself. For some people this can take years to figure out and we change our priorities and our interests till we get it right and things just feel good. If people or places do not feel good, you try to fit in rather than belong. The people that are meant to be in our life will accept us unconditionally and without effort. You only truly belong to yourself, so learn to be authentic in who you are and what you want in life.

I learned so many lessons on my way to Happy. I now live life from a different perspective of love and joy. I am grateful for everything I have and all that is a part of life. I choose my people carefully and live my life passionately. I am content yet keep pushing myself forward. I know I have a message to share, and I have received many compliments of inspiration. I know that my lessons are not my lessons alone. If I can help others to minimize their experience or have acceptance in their journey, then I am happy. I am not about preaching and have learned my place to ask permission. I listen to understand and comprehend. I have learned to be at peace with my decisions and others. I have learned how to walk away and not allow other people's moods to affect me at all. It is like sharing a bubble of light protecting me from the negatives around me. I am a realist, and I am a spiritual believer. I believe I have a purpose that is now only starting to take shape. I feel calm and peaceful.

The greatest lesson I learned was to not take anything personally. This is a big challenge for so many people. I get it. I did it for years. It made me feel less worthy, never enough and extremely emotional, and I held on to unhealthy relationships longer than I should have. I did not realize I was trapped so hard in this place until I got out. I realized that we all make decisions and choices based on our needs, wants and past experiences. Manipulation and blame are tools used to keep people from leaving or as a way of sabotaging relationships. The problem is that some people do it consciously; for others, it is an unconscious way of life based on their upbringing and all they know how to live or parent. When I finally got all the lessons of letting go of my old ways, I became happy and made all the choices that best suit my life now.

For the first time, other than the birth of my children and the time I spend with them, I can say I am honestly HAPPY and joyful. I do not feel like my childhood was happy. There were moments of happiness throughout my life, but not like this. This is a happiness that people search to fill a void. It is something you can only find within yourself. I trust my decisions and they guide me to what I need in my life now. Forever is too far away, so live life with only gratitude and not with expectations. Most people do not know what happiness feels like. They keep chasing others to fulfill their happiness, expecting it to be returned, not realizing it has always been within themselves. I did that, and I know it does not work. The more you give to the wrong people, the less you get. They steal your love and your happiness. You only receive true love when you unconditionally give it to yourself.

Joy is different than happiness. Happiness is a feeling deep inside based on what is happening around you. Our circumstances can define the happiness we feel. Joy is the attitude we live each day by.

Joy is the way we define the way we live, our peace, our love, and our gratitude. It is a daily way of grateful living. We take in stride the challenges of what we can endure. We understand that many things are out of our control, but because JOY comes from within, we create acceptance for everything that is. It is an internal attitude that takes ownership of all that we have. Joy is a component of learning to be authentic.

Happiness comes from allowing external forces to control our lives. We allow the reactions and emotions of others to shift our emotions from the outside world. Happiness is temporary and determined by how we feed the life we want. Happiness comes from a need to belong to something or someone's approval or validation that we are worthy of acceptance.

When you have the choice to live with joy or happiness, choose Joy every time. Joy will bring you happiness, and happiness does not always bring you Joy.

Everything in life changes, including us. Never expect the person you were at 20 will be the same person you will be at 40 or 60. Relationships change, and friendships shift. You may outgrow people, or they will outgrow you. Life just happens. The people that are meant to be in your life will always find their way back to you. The people that are not will find the door out.

Do not take for granted the people who have helped you through your tough times. They may not be there the next time you need them. When you learn to be true to your authentic self, your connections will transform, and so will you.

- You will learn that if you give others the power over your happiness, it will only ever come from an external source until you find the joy within.
- You will learn you do not need to trade your authenticity for attachments. The right people will find and love you as you are.
- You will learn to let go of the past and enjoy the moment without expectations.
- You will learn that when you follow your heart, good things happen. Trust the process.
- You will learn that you can live life on your terms.

Life is all about how you see the world. Allow your mindset to align with the life you deserve. Keep moving forward; nothing changes by looking back or returning to old habits and patterns that no longer serve you for the greater good. Believe in yourself because only YOU have the capacity to make your life better.

THE OLDER WE GET, the tougher we become. We are tougher and wiser from all the lessons and experiences we have endured.

We no longer listen to people's opinions or judgement because most people do not like themselves.

We no longer collect red flags from a relationship. Instead, we start looking for true colors.

The older we get, the more we know what true love feels like. It is that one person who will stop their world to be beside you in your need.

Everything has its own timing, and everything works out the way it is meant to.

It is not that people are afraid of commitment or love, but afraid of old pain, old triggers, and their own insecurities.

We realize that you can only really count on yourself and that independence is a gift and common sense is rare.

Not everyone will treat you how they want to be treated but expect you to treat them respectfully.

That life is not fair or equal, and it never will be. Take nothing in life for granted because, in a heartbeat, it can all be gone.

Remember each moment and day is a gift; the best memories are not about the event but the people you shared it with.

Self-love and self-care are different for everyone, but it is proof that you are always worthy of yourself. Life is not about learning to fit in but learning to accept yourself.

Everyone has a trauma story, but not everyone chooses to hold on to it forever. Instead, they choose to live their life, not their story.

You can never escape yourself so learn how to make peace with your past.

You can complain about your life or choose to change it. There are always resources available. You can choose to learn from them or regret them later. Either way, it is a choice.

Success is different for everyone; in the end happy people have fewer regrets.

Time is the most valuable thing you can give someone and the most treasured after it is gone.

Your determination and motivation are the only things that get you on the right path. It is about hard work, not what you have been given in life, but how you earn it.

Healing

Healing is a journey that can be scary and uncertain. Everyone has some form of healing they need to do but understanding it and surrendering to it are the challenges. Healing is a discovery of your needs and a letting go of the ties that bind your heart or even your soul. You cannot heal from the pain if you are unwilling to discover or uncover it.

Healing comes with the price of letting go of the past and forgiving everything that was out of your control or you were unconsciously aware of. It is about accepting what was and allowing the present to be all there is. It is about self-discovery of everything you did not know or did not understand and the ability to move forward. We need to heal the one that got hurt, abandoned, or never felt good enough. Heal the child that was bullied and teased. The one that felt like they never belonged and the one that stood alone.

Healing is letting go of every relationship you wanted to work out differently but did not. You may hold special memories in your heart for a long time. Let them be memories of a life you once enjoyed. Do not keep playing the victim to your past or keep wondering why people change or do not love you or stay connected.

Everyone and everything will change over time, and everything dies, so a new rebirth can happen. This is you. An improved version of you comes alive and embraces the world with knowledge from a unique perception. You can only do this from a healed version of yourself.

When we live by the rule of perfectionism and hold on to "I will be happy when" phrases, we need to figure out the real question. By whose standards is something perfect, and how will you know when you get there? Did you grow up in a society where you thought someone wanted perfection out of you? It was not perfection at all but a misinterpretation of just wanting better or believing you could achieve more. Parents and society understand there is no perfection in that case. It is important that you keep chasing your dreams and goals, but life is not about being right or perfect; it is about the many lessons we learn along the way. The standard of perfection will create disappointment because you will never be happy with the results. You cannot create long-lasting internal or external perfection as it is only ever going to be temporary. Healing from perfectionism can be harder when you feel you constantly compare or judge yourself by someone else's standards. Let go and just love and accept yourself for who you are right now, including your flaws, unconditionally.

Letting go of perfectionism and believing everything you went through to get to this place of healing was a lesson, giving you purpose and strength. Let go of the pain and the trauma so you find an inner peace that only you can heal. You cannot heal by focusing on past regrets and resentments. You can only heal by allowing yourself or others forgiveness.

Having emotional triggers from our past shows us both how far we have come and how far we must go. Healing triggers from our past can feel like an overwhelming sensation, an uncertainty of emotions deep inside. Healing from our triggers is about learning to let go and trust the universe, and the place you are in is safe. The reminder that you are where you belong. It is about learning to fall forward into trust. Time heals.

When a trigger comes up, breathe, and remember you survived it then and will survive it now. You were strong enough to get through it. You will be strong enough to get through anything. A trigger is not about the situation but the emotions and feelings behind it. A memory flashback that was created by emotions attached to it. Part of your past, not your present or your future.

Let it go, and know you are safe. Let it go, and know you are loved. Let it go and forgive yourself. Let it go and fall forward to your future. Your own self-healing will bring you to a place of unconditional love for yourself and compassion for others.

Heal the inner child by giving yourself the love you want most.

Heal the inner child by allowing the playful side to come out.

Heal the inner child with acceptance and the ability to just show up with unconditional love.

Part of our internal healing comes when we ease the feelings of shame (I am bad) to guilt (I did bad). We shame ourselves into believing that our choices and decisions from the past have made us bad parents, partners, annoying children, or unreliable friends. We allow others to shame us for who they expected us to be rather than who we are. People push their expectations and conditions on loving or accepting each of us. Everyone makes mistakes, and we learn from them to create better relationships in all aspects of our life. We shame ourselves when we do not feel worthy enough of love and belonging. We shame ourselves for all the things we do not know or understand. We shame ourselves for all the love we did not get or receive from the people we wanted.

Guilt comes from knowing we did the best we could and still made mistakes and errors in our judgement. My guilt says, "I made a mistake, learned from it, and forgive myself." I wanted to raise my children a certain way, but due to circumstances, I chose a path that did not allow this alignment. Guilt can be choosing to stay in a harmful or hurtful relationship because you are afraid of hurting someone else or because you are afraid of rejection or fear of abandonment. These are triggering responses from earlier in your childhood or early relationships.

When we put the blame on others for how we were parented, raised, or even in our relationships, we become powerless in our own healing. We stay stuck in past patterns of helplessness without taking ownership. We are now in control of our thoughts, feelings, and healing. Blaming comes from comparing the life we wanted instead of the life we had, whether by choice or circumstance. Healing is always by choice, but you must be willing to accept the lessons and forgive yourself or someone else.

When we can surrender to our past and let it go, we can move forward to a better life. When we can surrender to our expectations of life to a place of gratitude, life changes. When you can surrender your ego to just live life freely, you can create a world of fulfillment.

We surrender our heart when we become fully present and in love with someone. We become so vulnerable, allowing each of us to share our most intimate thoughts and feelings. We surrender what we thought life should be to an acceptance of what life is. When we learn to surrender, we allow others and ourselves to just be as we are at the moment. When we can hold space for someone in their place, they feel safe. Willing to open and share their most intimate fears and secrets. Ask for permission to be in their space, hug them and let them choose between silence or talking. Honor what they need at the moment.

The only way through Guilt and Shame is forgiveness of Self.

Guilt-free living

WE ALL HAVE past issues that make us feel guilty for the things we did or did not do. Yet we cannot go back and change the past, so we figure out how to deal with the shame or guilt with inner work. It takes a lot of self-reflection and ownership to come to terms with it and let it go with the thinking of "it is what it is" (or was). I cannot change what happened. I cannot change who I was or who someone else was in my life. I may not have always made the best decisions, but I did the best I could, or they did the best they could. Sometimes we can justify our choices and actions were not as good as they should have been, but generational trauma is handed down. It was worst for the generation before us, and they think they are doing better than how they were treated.

Each generation tries to improve from how they grew up. Sometimes the pendulum swings too far the other way and creates an imbalance of parents giving in and creating entitled children, never having appreciation or work ethic. We must get back to balanced parenting of working together. We need to teach the basics of learning to live within our means. So, later in life, you can still afford your lifestyle without relying on others to fill the void of your financial, emotional, and social needs.

Shame makes you feel like you are a bad person. Guilt is you did something wrong.

I let go of shame when I realized I did the best I could. I am a good person but loved the wrong person for too long. I had a lifetime of lessons to learn in one relationship. I felt guilt for my decisions in my life and parenting. I could not change them, so I had to let those feelings go for me. I finally realized I could live a happy life, and hopefully, my children would understand that I was on a learning curve in my own life. I made the decisions I thought best at that time, not realizing the consequences or the impact. I think in the end they learned lessons that they may have never learned either.

I had to let go of the past to enjoy my future. I realized that no matter how much past guilt I was holding on to, it would not change what happened in the past. It is not up to me to make my children have acceptance of the past. It is their choice to forgive or let go.

As I learned to love myself unconditionally and accept who I was and who I am now, I learned to let go. It was what it was, and life is what it is. You learn from your mistakes, and you grow from them. It took me a long time to let go of my enabling patterns of wanting to keep the peace and not upset anyone. I realized I could not make anyone happy, especially if I was not happy. Now that my children have grown up, I decided to make the right choices for me to improve my future. I am not the same person I was at 20, 30, or 40 years old. My needs are different, and so is my life.

I learned that I do not need to fit in and love my own company. I love positive people, have similar values, are genuine and have strong boundaries. (Something I lacked for years). I learned that my worth is not negotiable with anyone, and at 50 years old, I am capable of whatever I choose. I have worked for everything I have and appreciate the people, support, and all that I have. So, when I make my choices, it is about what is best for me and my life. I no longer feel guilt for choosing what is best for me, rather than upsetting someone else. This is my life, and I will live it guilt-free, with the underlying rule of doing no harm to others.

Guilt-free living is about taking care of my needs first, it is not selfish and there is no harm to others. I can walk away from the people or places that no longer serve a purpose in my life. I can detach from a toxic person yet still be kind and generous with boundaries when I choose to have contact. I choose to accept people for who they are, which also allows me to let them go when it is necessary. I do not need to give unsolicited advice to fill up my own cup and share my experiences to justify my past decisions and resolutions. I no longer have a need or want to fit in with anyone.

Guilt-free living still comes with the consequences of making the wrong choices. You are never free from the consequences of your actions or your decisions. Not everyone will accept or understand your choices, and they may affect others' lives differently than yours. When my dad passed away, I gave my son a choice of seeing him for a visit one last time. I allowed him to make the right decision for him, as he must live with the consequences of his decisions. As he thought about it for a couple of days and the time was getting close, he said, "my last visit with papa was the best, and I choose to remember him that way." Great, I am glad he came to that conclusion on his own without guilt from me, or anyone, especially himself. He will never regret it because he made a choice he could live comfortably with. It was a long drive home just to watch his papa die when he had just gone through the passing of his own father five months prior. In the end they had a funny laugh and shared a delightful story through facetime, which was a perfect closure for both.

Not everyone will accept your choices or your decisions. They do not understand your why, nor do they have you. You owe very few people an explanation in life unless it also affects their life.

Choose to communicate when necessary so you both can make a guilt-free decision.

You may always have guilt or resentment from the past, but letting it go due to an inability to change allows you to free yourself from being powerless. It allows you to move forward with a more conscious mind of the decisions you choose and the lives that will be affected. Guilt-free living is not only what is good for you, but all those involved because the awareness and mindfulness are both completely free.

Acceptance

THE ONLY WAY I realized I could love myself wholeheartedly was through acceptance. Acceptance, that I am worthy of love. Acceptance, that I did the best I could. Acceptance of loving myself right now exactly as I am right now. No more chasing joy and seeking my value in other people's validation.

When you create an understanding that everything in life happens for a reason, you can let go of the why and the victimized role we have each played to keep us stuck in a guilt or shame spiral. Some people truly were victims of circumstance, and some maintained the victimized roles longer than necessary. When we take ownership of our emotions, we start to learn and accept that we can make our life as great or as painful as we need it to be. I can walk away from the people or places that no longer serve my presence or my future goals. Everything you went through in your life contributed to the person you are today.

When I shifted my beliefs about what my partner's addiction was teaching me, I was able to understand it was never about me. I was just a player in the game. I sacrificed years of my life for knowledge. I was always confident and secure within myself, but I was naïve to many world issues and relationships. I had so much love to give and just wanted it so much in return that I was willing to go all in every time for the affection that was given. I allowed myself to feel rejection and be second best, thinking the crumbs I received were the best it would get. When we put others on a pedestal, it will break. When we give others all our love and admiration, it will eventually crumble because perfection only decreases. All the things that make us question our worth make us re-evaluate our priorities and values.

I learned to accept myself as I am, to love me now. Not 30 pounds lighter, not when I had more money or the perfect relationship. Love me now! I started to accept who I am at this moment. It was up to me to create a better life if I wanted a better life. It was up to me to set my goals and go after them by aligning my life according to my outcome. The more I accepted myself, my worth became non-negotiable with others. I no longer care about other people's opinions. Let them judge what they do not know. They never walked in my shoes or felt my emotions. They belong to me. They may have had similar scenarios, but I am not them, and they are not me. Most people only judge through the lens of their own experience and values what they would have done in your situation. I realized I had created many resiliencies to have the strength to endure the fight and become the survivor.

I have accepted everyone has their own journey. I can guide them, but I cannot make their choices. I can give suggestions, but it is up to each person to do their own work. I accepted that my ex-partner and others were only trying to meet their own needs. I needed to let go of my ego and accept that how I allowed my feelings to grasp every hurtful rejection or words was based on my interpretation. I freed myself when I accepted what others did was about them and had nothing to do with me. I could walk in and out of a room and not allow the mood shift of others to control my self-worth or drain my energy. I regained my power.

Acceptance comes from your own healing journeys. The ability to take ownership of everything that happened in our life was for a reason. A place where the blame falls away, and you accept you did the best you could at the time. Despite their bad choices, your parents are the only ones who raised you better than they were. You finally understand they were only humans and make bad decisions themselves. Acceptance that life was as it was meant to be, the good, the bad and the ugly. That everything happened for a reason, to bring you to this moment in your life right now. The only way you can learn to have acceptance is by letting go of the pain of the past and stopping living by fear and anxiety of the future. Start living each day as the gift it is. Love and happiness follow acceptance. I accepted that my journey was to bring me to a place to help others create boundaries in their life and learn to love themselves worthy to know they are enough just as they are.

At some point we learn acceptance of ourselves and others for exactly who they are. We drop the expectations and conditions we place on others for them to be a certain way. We release placing our values and beliefs on them and just accept them as they are. It does not mean we have to agree with them, believe their point, their lies, or even like them. We just accept they are the way they are for reasons that are beyond our control. People are doing their best in their environment, their conditioning, and how they were raised.

Society has adopted a new way of thinking. If someone is toxic, you may unfriend them and walk away. They blame unequal energy on one person being toxic. It is up to us how we perceive toxicity and allow others to drain our energy when we are not in a frame of resilience. This usually happens when we have different values, beliefs, or a different world model and how we view the difference between right and wrong.

When we learn to accept ourselves as imperfect, we can then accept others as imperfect and a constant work in progress. We can only start to love ourselves unconditionally when we dismiss the need for perfection and control. We unleash the need to fill the voids of life and seek fulfillment of internal joy instead of chasing external happiness, which only lasts for a brief period before we seek the next thing to fulfill our need.

When we understand that people want to be seen and heard, we create a different reference point in how we show up in our own authenticity. True acceptance is when someone else's actions or reactions no longer control you. Your emotions are not managed by someone's life. You no longer have a desire to change or fix someone. You do not place unrealistic expectations or conditions on a friendship or relationship. Your boundaries can be accepted and met with integrity and respect. You are not responsible for anyone in this life, except for your children till they are old enough to become responsible for themselves. At some point they will learn from the natural consequences of their decisions and actions. By taking away someone's responsibility, we become enablers of their behavior or happiness. Therefore, we are not accepting who they are in this world. You may not agree with them, but it is their journey, and we all get to choose our own path.

True acceptance must start with accepting yourself. *You are perfectly imperfect.* Perfection is unattainable and has a negative effect because you diminish your own worth, which leaves you to feel unworthy and never enough. Learn to love yourself with all your unique beauty. Love yourself unconditionally, no matter the circumstances or the influences of others. When you accept yourself fully, no one can break your confidence. Do not dull your shine to make others less uncomfortable in your presence or your dreams.

When we show up authentically in our everyday life with consistency, people learn to trust us. They learn that we have integrity and accountability. They learn they can also show up with their authentic self without judgement.

Understanding someone is the key to having healthy relationships and boundaries. Understand the person's characteristics and attributes. Do not try to change them to suit your needs or expectations or put conditions on any friendship. Unfortunately, most people only want to accept people who are like them and describe everyone else as toxic. Wearing a mask that creates a false persona has become a survival technique for many people that feel unworthy of belonging or being loved. They have denied themselves the risk of being authentic due to past circumstances that have put them in a constant feeling of judgement, through self or peers. We are harder on ourselves based on our childhood experiences. If you were abused, bullied, or teased as a child, chances are you grew up trying to prove your worthiness for the ability to belong or fit in. If you had a less attentive or less responsive parent to your needs, you might have felt unloved and never enough. In these situations, it was never about being less important, but the people mistreating you. But our perspective internalizes the situations as if everyone is against us. Children bully to cover up their own insecurities in their life. It gives them significance. Adults or parents may be less responsive or attentive to one child's needs or wants because they have many children, and the one child may be able to fend for themselves easier. Or the parents worked and had a lot to do at the end of the day. They were trying to fit everything in. There is never an excuse for abuse and neglect. Sometimes it can be generational trauma episodes passed down; no one knows or understands how to genuinely love themselves or another person, and everyone loses.

You must take responsibility for your choices at a certain time in your life. You can no longer play the victim of the bully card. You can no longer go through life feeling abandoned by a situation from the past. All those unfortunate situations have given you great gifts of life experience. The greatest lesson you can teach is to never make anyone else feel the way you felt. Build your character strength based on some of your unwanted identities and experiences. At some point, you need to create a self-development journey, to grow and be better than you were the year before. Life is a continuous learning strategy.

I am Enough

I AM ENOUGH.
> I tell myself.
> Looking in the mirror,
> Trying to convince the person I see before me.

I AM ENOUGH.
> To stand tall in my beliefs and in my values.
> To believe in love and purpose.
> To acknowledge my mistakes from the past.

I AM ENOUGH.
> To share my voice,
> To make my message clear,
> To be seen and heard just as I am.

I AM ENOUGH.

Let me shine with the love I give and receive.
Let me live my life's purpose
And never look back.

I AM ENOUGH.
And so are You.
Let your beautiful smile glow.
And your heartbeat with passion.

I AM ENOUGH.
Starts with loving yourself.
Let go of your old story.
And know that worthiness begins from within!

Rising Strong

To Rise Strong, we must fall. Falling is a process that teaches us how to build resilience both emotionally and physically. Our breakdowns are a blessing in disguise. We create breakthroughs at those times. When we learn to acknowledge the situation, get curious about the emotions we feel, the triggers that are released, and accept that something is wrong. Breakdowns are a part of growth opportunities to teach you a better way to live.

Part of my breakdown realized that I was in the wrong relationship and did not like the person I had become or the parenting process I was going through. My life was in chaos, and I struggled with my identity. I realized I was living someone else's life. This was not the life I wanted anymore. Sometimes we realize that we have invested too much time in someone else, and all our values have been sidetracked. We get lost in meeting someone else's visions and needs.

When my life was in the middle of a breakdown, I was emotionally exhausted and feeling lost. Everything was falling apart, and I did not know what to do. I had to figure out my new path in life aligned with my new goals and the life I wanted to lead. As my children started to live their own life and create their own destinies, I realized I was now in charge of my future. My relationship was over, and I had to pick myself up and keep going. In the middle of the breakdown, I realized this was my breakthrough. In the same year I lost me, my relationship, my ex-husband, and my father. It turned my life upside down, yet at the same time, it made me appreciate everything I thought I was missing. I started looking at life from a new perspective. I started living life with gratitude and appreciation for each day and each person I met. I started to follow my heart, living with passion and adventure. I started honoring myself and my emotions. I started enjoying life again. I gave up on ego and entitlement. I went through a transformation of self-improvement. It was the greatest feeling of my life. I now feel grateful for everything and look at life from a different perspective every day.

I learned to cultivate consciousness. To be aware of my surroundings and be conscious of my thoughts and the language I use daily. I released my expectations of others and my own insecurities that I had projected on others or myself due to fear and judgement. I am now conscious of what I do in life and the ripple effect it will create for myself or others involved. Most people go through life without awareness of consciously making decisions that may change the course of their life or have a ripple effect on those around them.

Fear and ego keep you stuck in your own head. You create assumptions rather than working through them with communication and the story you tell yourself. The fear of judgment from others is really the fear and insecurities of yourself. Being conscious about your relationship with yourself is important to your relationships with others. Your thoughts control the way you speak to others and yourself. It affects your decisions to act and push yourself beyond your comfort level. By cultivating consciousness, you can make better choices and propel yourself to the next level of your life. You become a better partner, parent, and friend. You can let go of ego and create empowerment for yourself and others around you. Your survival mode relaxes, and you live life more passionately with a focus on an end goal.

I went through this gratitude process and a story I tell myself, which I still do as a daily practice. It has transformed my life. In the beginning, as I became conscious of shifting my thoughts and behaviors, I would catch myself in a story several times a day. Eventually, this transformation process became natural until I no longer did it. Now I can see and recognize when others are in their story. Being able to call Bullshit on yourself is very empowering and a level of growth. It means that we take our power back. We start to live life on our terms. Your relationships become healthier because we no longer create assumptions for others. We start focusing on ourselves, our thoughts, and our feelings. As we heal, we get clarity in our own life rather than concentrating on others' judgement.

We all learn from the tough times, the sad times, the struggles, and the challenges of life. My mother always said, *"if you are going through hell, keep on going."* Self-determination gets you through, knowing there is always a light on the other side of darkness. Never let anything get in your way. When the fire is hot, walk-through hell like you own the place. Never let your fears stop you from becoming who you are meant to be in life. These challenges are only there to test your strength and build your resiliency. They are to prove to you that you are smarter, braver, and stronger than you think. Dig deep and find the fighter, the warrior, and the survivor. WE all have it in us. It is up to you to pull it out! Accept that life will give you challenges, but it is up to you if you decide to live in hell or walk through it with pride.

We all have a warrior inside of us. It is the part of us that we draw our strength and courage from, the part that keeps us fighting for everything we believe in. Being a warrior and a survivor takes a great mindset and a divine spirit. The unstoppable force pushes you to get through anything with the vulnerability of not knowing what is on the other side of the challenges you will face or the demons you must slay. It is not about the fight of the warrior. It is the wisdom and the courage to keep fighting and moving forward no matter what life throws your way. It is the spirit inside that keeps you alive.

You do not always realize the inner strength of your mind until you must rise above all the heartache and the stresses of life that you have been through. All the struggles you think are meant to break you give you inner power and strength to push you through to the next level. They are not to make you weak but to build further resistance for the moments when you need them the most.

You are a fighter; you are a warrior, and you are a survivor! If you allow your mind to take over in times of weakness, you will never feel your inner strength. Those times you were made to push back and keep fighting harder with your mind than ever before. Do not let the demons take over. You are stronger than you believe, but only you can do the work. Only you can train your mind to be stronger than any emotion attached to an outcome.

Keep fighting because you are worth it. You will always be more valuable than you ever realize.

Celebrate your wins and your losses

It is important to celebrate every victory we have. Every milestone is a step in the right direction. We forget that it is important to celebrate our losses as well. Each loss is not a failure but also a step in the right direction. It means that whatever was holding us back has now made room for a more aligned future. All the losses or what we look at as failures are blessings. If they did not collapse at our feet, we may never be ready or forced to take a chance due to fear.

Most relationships end because we are no longer in tune with one another. Our values are different than we first saw them. We have different goals, and despite the inner knowledge that it is time to let go and move forward, we struggle with the relationship's failure and mourn its loss. Most people stay in a job they hate or a relationship far longer than they should. If one person is unhappy, chances are they both are. Plus, if you hate your job, it is not good for you, the people you serve, or the company you work for. It becomes stressful. No one benefits.

We need to celebrate all the wins and all the losses. Both give you lessons in your life. The losses give you the biggest lessons. It is better to learn what is no longer right for you and your life than to stay stuck and unhappy for many years to come. That serves no purpose.

What if you stayed in a job for 20 years, knowing you never followed your passion? It is all about fear! Fear of success and fear of failure. Yet if you lose your job, a new opportunity presents itself. You may have stayed in a relationship for 20 years because you believed that this is as good as it gets. You assumed this was love because you have never had anything better. Then that person leaves or passes away, and you find that you had wasted time and learned lessons in an unfulfilled life. Instead, you could have been loving life with someone that loved you and treated you better than anyone else had in the past.

Do not fear the losses. Celebrate them! They are your wins!

New level new devil

As we start to transition our way through life and relationships, we have uncertainty about everything around the next corner. We have no expectations of what adventures lie ahead. We are willing to take a chance on whatever comes next. Sometimes we must face a new level and a new devil, so we can grow and heal. So we can learn more lessons. We can become more independent at a new level, searching for new growth opportunities, compassion and understanding. A new devil is about healing from the old triggers or learning to deal with new people and situations that may bring up new challenges or uncomfortable decisions. Going through the transition process may not be easy, but there is always a lesson.

We all have transitions in life that take us to the next phase or the next chapter of our life. Sometimes this consists of a new relationship that can be a turning point from lost love and sadness to seeing the beauty in love and understanding. It shows you that when you thought the past pain was too much to bear, it was only a moment in time. New love teaches you that you deserve to be loved, and sometimes the love you thought you had, was not the love you really needed.

Transitions can be temporary, short, and unpredictable. They can range from a new job, a new friend, a new living arrangement, or a new partner. Sometimes grown children coming home to stay for a while is transitioning them from one life stage to another. Transitions in life are important for our growth. It is a place of acceptance from what once was to a place of now. When we miss the transitions or do not understand them going into a situation, we may get caught up emotionally when we realize that it was not as we expected. When we expect a situation or relationship to last forever, we stop putting 100% effort in and take it for granted. Have an acceptance of the transition as growth and the phase of getting you to the next chapter of your life.

When I started my new relationship, I came across my "old story" several times. I would sit and ask myself, *"what is the story you are telling yourself?"* What are your facts? What are your assumptions? When we are willing to be transparent with another person and clarify our values and expectations of standards in a relationship, the relationship will have trust, honesty, and communication. You are laying down bricks for your future foundations. Not a bed of broken glass, with avoidance and dishonesty. When our past triggers us, we understand that sometimes the triggers have nothing to do with the person in front of you but the person inside you. Blame is easy and chickenshit. You never have to take ownership of the things you never healed from. Blame comes from fear. Fear of rejection and fear of success. Yet when you are scared, you do not feel you are equipped to handle the joy. Therefore, we start sabotaging our joy. You are responsible for acknowledging the difference between past triggers and current situations. When I released my insecurities from the past, the transitions became easier. Everything begins to flow with calmness and ease, including me. I was open to new experiences in life.

Fall forward

ONE THING I have learned in my lifetime of relationships is I need to go back before I can move forward. I need to know that I have done all I could do in that relationship for me and everyone involved. Although I have had some regrets about returning to a situation, I have also learned more lessons that helped me move on and become a better version of myself. I can step away knowing that although I was all in at one point, I was also ready to be all out. I could see the issues more clearly, making it easier to move on without blame, judgment or hate. It simply had run its course and it was time for something new, even if that new is just time to find and redefine me.

Everyone wants to be loved and belong somewhere. We want to love someone for their good qualities. Sometimes, we see the red flags and start collecting them in the relationship for the potential of the person or relationship. This holds us back, remembering the enjoyable times or the few moments of true love and laughter. Remember, walking away from any situation that no longer makes you happy and fulfilled is okay. Everything has an expiration date.

Take time for yourself when you are in the transformation stage.

Pay attention to the updated version of you coming out versus going into a relationship. Your core may be the same, but your tolerance of acceptance may differ.

I finally decided to leave a relationship with someone who didn't see my value anymore. I was able to start to fall forward. I knew going back was no longer an option. We both changed, everyone does after ten years. We grew apart instead of together. I was only able to help someone that was willing to help themselves and work as a partner. The partnership was gone, making me realize that it was never equal or fair. I was able to walk away with my dignity and my integrity. I felt like I was the queen of my own world. This was my time to shine.

As I started to fall forward in life, I became happier. I realized how important it was to become your own best friend by loving and accepting yourself unconditionally. I could enjoy my own company without feeling lost, sad, and lonely. I started to reach for my own goals without feeling like I was sacrificing my life for someone else's. I started to understand my own values and why my relationships did not work out. I realized that it was up to me to create my own happiness. So, I started falling forward to everything I wanted. I took the time to learn, read and take a course. I made a vision board of everything I wanted to manifest in my life. Then over the next three years, it started to come true. I bought my dream car, a 1998 Corvette. I took my children on a vacation that I promised them when they were young. I reconnected with the man I fell in love with 30 years ago. We live in a peaceful country place by the lake, and now we are happily married. I fell forward to a better life because I knew I deserved it. We all do!

We all fail and feel like a failure, but these are a part of our lessons to learn. Stop falling back into the same patterns with the same type of people. Fall forward into a new and exciting life. Fall forward into a love that makes you come alive with passion. Fall forward into a future that leads you to your goals. Fall forward into all the things that life offers with new experiences and new possibilities. You were never made to stay stuck. You were never made to live the same day repeatedly. You were made to fall forward, taking all your greatness to the next level.

If you go back into a situation that you have outgrown, remember it is only to realize that there is more to life than anything from the past. It is up to you to create a more compelling future, and the universe will show you a better way. Take a chance to see what lies ahead because you have already lived looking behind. When you fall, make sure you are falling forward into your best life.

Chapters

WE ALL GO through new chapters of life. Sometimes at the most unexpected times. When the chapter ends, and we are not ready for the next one to begin, that's when we appreciate our transitions.

When we look back at the chapters of our life, we realize every chapter has brought us to our place. It all starts to make sense. You realize that all the experiences and the heartbreaks you had were like the pieces in a puzzle. We cannot miss a chapter, and we should not go back and repeat them. Each chapter is a life lesson. Take time with your chapters, so you fully understand each as a gift. Each chapter has meaning to your life. Some will be scary, full of love, sorrow, exciting and painful. Each is about creating your worth and your best version in life.

You are the book, this is your story, and you are the author. Too often, we think we cannot leave a relationship, our job, and old friendships, and we are just walking through life with the same scenario of a "same book, different page" attitude. Is that a book you want to read? If every page had the same writing, the same outcome and the same dull emotions, would you take the time to read the book? Chances are NO. So why do you live your life that way?

You live your life this way because it's comfortable. You do not have to look fear in the eye. You do not have to live life with the uncertainty of knowing what is coming next. You can fall back to your old excuses and old patterns just to stay in your comfort zone when things get tough. You never have to take a chance of feeling the old pain with a new love.

New chapters in life are about excitement, passion, adventure, and the uncertainty of what will happen next. You get to live life to the fullest. You get to experience new adventures and make new memories with new people, places, and emotions. New chapters are new beginnings, and you can start writing yours whenever you choose.

We all have a story that has defined our past. We all have a story we can be the victim in. We all have a story we are the hero in, and we all have a story we no longer identify with. Learn to divorce your old story and marry the truth.

The truth is you are only as good as the story you keep replaying in your head.

The truth is you are only keeping yourself stuck by allowing those stories to label or define you.

The truth is there is more to you than any story from your past.

The truth is you define your own limitations and beliefs.

The truth is we all go through the pain and suffering at some point.

The truth is you can write a new chapter in your story any moment you want to.

The truth is you are the only one in charge of your state, emotions, and the meaning in your life.

The truth is you have more power than you believe in changing your life.

The truth is you are in control.

Now is the time to write a new truth and a new story. Stop reliving the same story and the same patterns. Honor your own life instead of living someone else's dreams. You cannot have a better life reliving the same chapter over. You get to decide... Which book do you want to read? Which book do you want to write?

You are the author, and you can rewrite a new chapter whenever you want.

Choices

I GREW up with the belief system that "we all have choices." Sometimes we make choices in our life that have huge consequences for not only ourselves but the others around us. As parents, any choice we make can directly affect our children. Unfortunately, there is such a duality problem of wanting to live your own life yet making choices not conducive to the needs of our children. We see it every day in parents who want to have a life of partying and drugs, and yet it is the children that suffer the most. This suffering takes place immediately in a direct form of behaviors. Other times it takes years to surface through a child's own addictions or choices as they get older.

In relationships we make choices about the people we want to associate with, long or short term. Sometimes we make choices we feel are right at the moment but may not be healthy in the long term. When we become so overwhelmed with "love emotions", we do not see the red flags of the person or the relationship. We keep trying thinking life will get better. We put off our decisions to leave a relationship, a job, a friendship, or a situation so long that we feel like we no longer have a choice. It seems impossible to find a solution. We create a position of helplessness. We endure the decisions from our past longer than we need or want to. We feel we just do not have the strength or resources to make a different choice.

When the time is right, we either continue to suffer the repercussions of our decisions and actions or make a new choice to align our life with a better direction. It is ***"in the moments that you think you have no choice you must make a new decision." -Tony Robbins***

Your everyday choices make up your everyday life. The people you surround yourself with will either hold you back or take you to the next level. They will bring bitterness or happiness to your life. Some people choose to live in survival mode waiting for the next explosion of their life. Others think life should come to them and provide them will all their necessities. Most people live day to day, not knowing how to prepare for the rest of their life. No idea of the differences between priorities and pleasures. People have habits that they have developed as priorities. They feel helpless to change or improve their quality of life. If you are not happy in your life, make a change. You are the only one responsible for your choices. First, you must take ownership of your life.

*Each day we make choices that affect our life and those surrounding us. It is called the **Ripple Effect**. Ripples are created by our actions, our words, and our lifestyle. Everything we do has a natural ripple effect of natural consequences. Choose your choices consciously, for each person suffers or benefits from the **Ripple Effect**.*

The day I found myself

MOST PEOPLE GO through years of being stuck in old patterns, old beliefs, and a lack of identity. We get caught up in living what we feel as someone else's life. We feel lost in someone else's body and mind. Our life becomes so routine that we forget the direction of our goals and fall into habits with going to work, raising our children, and just getting by in survival mode each day. One day we realize we have had enough, and something must change.

When we feel stuck, we start looking for ways to change ourselves or our jobs. These are the easiest solutions; we believe we have the most control over when. However, the commitment to losing weight and going to the gym never seems sustainable. We lack that variety, passion, and fire in our life. We lost it in our relationship, so we seek to fill a void in other forms. The problem is we have given up so much of ourselves that we don't even know what we are passionate about anymore.

As my children grew up, I realized they didn't need me as much anymore. This felt like a huge loss in my identity. It is true what they say, "blink, and you miss it." My children no longer needed their mom for many things. I started having guilt and resentment for all the time I missed or was not the parent I wanted to be. Somehow life just became different. Knowing that I couldn't go back and change the past, I had to look at changing our life moving forward.

I went to therapy for at least a year. I cried many tears over what I felt my life had become. I did not see the red flags or signs of the emotional abuse I had my family in or how toxic I became due to these situations. I went for sessions with my children and learned their position. I realized that many times I did not listen when I should have or validated them. I did not listen or validate my own emotions and feelings when things did not feel right anymore. Therapy helped me find myself.

As I started to wake up from the unconscious chaos of my life, I realized I was no longer happy, and everything took more effort to keep the peace than it should have. I realized I would never be happy trying to make others happy long-term. I was on the way to finding my voice. When presented with an ultimatum of relationships between my spouse and my son. That was the day I found myself and my voice.

I went to the beach to think and ground myself. I walked, sat on a swing, listened to music, and had a good long cry about what my life had become and crumbled to. I thought about my life over the past ten years. I knew living this way was no longer an option, and I have 100 things to say that no longer could be contained to saving the peace I pretended I was creating. There was no peace, and there had not been for years. When I came back, we talked about the past ten years and the emotional harm that was caused. Not all of it was blamed as I took ownership. For the first time in years, I found my voice. The broken glass I had gently walked on for years had cleared a path, and I spoke my mind. I was mad, hurt, and DONE. I had enough of living this way. I figured at this point, I had nothing to lose in my life. I wanted a better life and did not know what that would be, but anything was better than how I lived.

That was the beginning of the end of our relationship. Once you give someone an ultimatum, it will end soon. A month passed and nothing got better except my voice was stronger. I was finding a new me. The one that I knew I had hit a point of no return. I had enough! I knew there was more to life and living like this. A month later he was gone. My world crashed for a while as I grieved the loss of our relationship, remembering the good and forgetting the bad. That is typical of relationships based on the addiction to love.

For a year after, we did not live together but continued to date and work on our relationship from a different state. I was a different person, and so was he. It was great for a period, but I could recognize the lies and emotional abuse again within a few months. I had to go back so I could go forward in my life. I knew there was one more lesson I had to learn but could not figure it out till it was over.

In that year I learned so much about myself. I had a year to figure out who I was and what I wanted out of my life. My daughter was at home but did her own thing. She was 17 and finding her way through friendships and life. I started to live life for myself, and my eyes were awakened to the relationship I was still trying to save and yet learning more about my direction for my future. I realized I was very capable of my own independence. I always knew I was, I just had to prove it again to myself. I was financially secure and had a new path in life.

I downsized my home and made changes to lead me to a better life. I went through the death of a relationship that no longer served me as I realized our values and goals were not aligned. This was followed by the death of my ex-husband (the father of my children) from lung cancer. Then five months later my father passed away after his right leg was amputated. The only thing I could control was the ending of my relationship. At the time it was both a relief and a loss. It was the only love I knew for the past 11 years, now it was gone.

I learned to BREATHE a little better as I started to release the past, having learned many lessons. I went through addiction, mental health issues, and suicide attempts with my partner. I raised two stepchildren and my two children. They all turned out to be great people I am proud of daily. They also learned many lessons along the way to make them strong, with the ability to set boundaries and know their worth.

Part of finding myself was reassuring myself that I am strong and independent. I have a beautiful heart and am willing to help others when they need me. I understand boundaries, mental health, addiction of a loved one, and narcissism that many do not realize. I fell in love with me again. I became passionate about what I do and who I am.

I learned to love and accept myself unconditionally. I learned to use my voice and ask for what I need and what I want. I learned to let go of the past and accept the lessons it gave me. I learned to question the stories I told myself, so I don't get caught up in my old beliefs and patterns. I let go of the expectations of others based on my old ego and control. I let go of others' opinions and judgments. Best of all, I also let go of taking anything personally. That is one of the biggest lessons I learned.

We are all just a work in progress trying to find our way to happiness. We lose our identity while becoming a spouse and raising children. Most of us do not realize it till we are too far and must find our way back. It is worth the lessons to finally be whole again. To find your purpose and realize you are in control of your own life. To take back your power and move forward knowing this is the new path for you. To let go of the person you were so you can become the person you are meant to be in all your grace and glory. To love and accept yourself, your own company, and everything you are. At the end of the day, you are the only person that must live with you. Learn how to talk to yourself like your own best friend and how to speak kindly to yourself.

Rebirth

Sometimes in life we are given opportunities for new chapters of rebirth. Just when we think the world is crashing down at our feet, we have two options. Play the victim or be the hero of your life.

Internally I died. I hid this all very well; chances are, no one ever saw or felt my pain. Everything happened all at once. The year of my loss was 2019. I lost three of my greatest loves. My father and my friend, the father of my children, died suddenly. My children's father had been battling lung cancer for a few years and was on borrowed time for a while. Everything changed suddenly in a week. I was thankful all three of us got to be by his side till the end. This was especially important for my children; they had mended relationships to be by his side from the past. In the last week, we exchanged our love in words while my daughter took it in. Understanding that just because we went our separate ways, it was never about them. That you can love someone and live your life the way you need. That we had the common love and respect for our children.

My father had cancer, but that was not what took his life. He had a leg amputation that went septic and could not fight it off. I remember talking to him on Sunday as he discussed his plans for

MAID (Medical Assistance in Dying). He was tired of the pain and could not do the fight anymore. Two days later he became indescribable after a fall out of bed. He could not talk and was quickly on a downward spiral of delusion and extreme pain. We stayed by his side for three days, watching the decline, afraid that he would pass at any time. It happened so fast, without the ability to have a conversation, it made goodbyes harder. I was proud of my daughter for having such compassion, love, and courage to stand by her father till the end and then her grandfather. I know the loss I felt. I know she has sorrow. She has not yet been released. I was there till the end; I saw my father take his last breath. I saw the change in his expression, the decrease in his breathing until he took the last one. It was heartbreaking.

I also lost the relationship with my best friend and my love. Eleven years of love, happiness, and challenges, but I was in it for the long haul. I stood by his addictions and mental health issues, dodging every red flag I could. I always figured the diamond in the rough I knew was inside would eventually come out. I saw some amazing qualities; we had both chemistry and commonality. At that time, he was my everything. Life decided it had a different plan for us and me.

Despite all my losses at once, I realized it was the biggest wake-up call life could have given me. It created a rebirth, and I decided to live in the mortality of peace. Living in love and passion for life every day. I took my children on the holiday I had promised them from their childhood. We experienced some of the greatest adventures of our life. We each got to fulfill a bucket list wish. Mine was a helicopter ride through the mountains. It was important for our bonding time, especially after the loss of their father. I decided I needed to start living as if there was no more tomorrow. I understood the secret of living in peace. I felt like I was given the gifts of gratitude that few understood. Something just clicked and has given me a massive shift in my message to the world. I live in gratitude for each moment. I have learned to let go of ego and see the world and people from an unfamiliar perspective and acceptance. I feel like I live each day in both happiness and peace, as I have never felt before.

So, when someone asked me, "did you ever have a near-death experience?" I said, "yes, I died internally" that year. My old life, my old ways, and my heart. But out of it came the best rebirth I could never have imagined. I live different, I love different, and I show up in the world different. The old me died, and the new me has the rest of my life.

Welcome to the person you are supposed to become to inspire the rest of the world.

A Hero's Journey

At some point in our life, we all must become our own hero, so we do not surrender to a life of victimization. At some point we must release everything that was so we can become everything we are meant to be. We need to realize that the hurt or harm caused by others stemmed from their own pain that was never dealt with.

Your soul's journey is about heartache, pain, fear, adversity, and resilience. It is about going through the hard stuff and challenges you thought were meant to break you so you could push through with fierce courage and become the person you are today. Life was never meant to be easy, and everyone has at least one story that has made them stronger because of the challenges they endured.

Throughout your journey you will be forced to go through the toughest decisions about dropping your armor to become vulnerable and authentic. Amor is there to protect you from getting hurt, but eventually, it harms you by not allowing your true self to unfold. You do not let anyone break the walls of your true self. We have kept our guard up to save ourselves from old hurt with new loves or carrying our insecurities to the next relationship. We guard against anyone seeing the vulnerable side of emotions, as that appears as a weakness to some. "We must be strong," we tell ourselves; "I can do it alone and do not need help from anyone." These are trauma responses. The truth is, we all need someone. We were not made to be strong always in the way we were taught. Inner strength comes when you can show up and be authentic, despite others' opinions of what strength or weakness is.

Adversity shows you opportunities for new growth by stepping out of your comfort zone and taking a chance. Fear becomes the monster inside of you that holds you back from trying new adventures, new paths, or new relationships. Fear holds you in situations longer than you should be because the fear of the unknown can be scarier than the pain you feel. Fear creates self-doubt and a feeling of unworthiness. Fear is the monster that makes you doubt your abilities and wear the armor of protection, shame, or guilt. The fear in you becomes toxic, and you start projecting those fears and insecurities onto others. Instead of dealing with your own toxicity and taking ownership, you begin projecting it onto others in the form of blame. Fear becomes the regrets for all the opportunities you missed. It becomes the resentment of not taking chances or walking away from people or situations that were never meant for you long term.

Some fear is necessary as it keeps us stable and evaluates situations before jumping in. As we learn to trust our instincts, we start to let go of the past's big fears and pain, so we can begin to find our bliss. Our bliss is our happy place. It's where we begin to feel at peace with the past, and we can make decisions for our future that aligns with who we are now. To get to this place of spiritual bliss, you must get to where you have had enough of the old ways or patterns that have kept you stuck and unhappy. A change takes place, and the death of your old life and old thinking must occur. You stop taking on the victim role of mentality and see the situation as a learning curve of experience, and a greater lesson is always present. You need to get out of your ego that keeps you thinking, "why me or poor me," and know it was about making you into the best version of yourself.

Your soul's journey is about slaying your dragons and your ego from within. It is about learning to love and accept yourself for who you are authentic. You let go of all the old versions of yourself from the past, especially the unfavorable ones. It is about learning new perspectives and being open to new challenges. Letting go of past regrets or pain others caused and realizing that was part of their learning process. You received valuable lessons from those people to last you a lifetime instead of feeling hurt, angry, and regretful. Feel it, release it, and let it go. Thank them for the journey. You become your own hero in the journey. You saved yourself from a life of victimization. You have slain your own dragons that kept you stuck in your own life of armor and toxic patterning behavior.

In every hero's journey we start as one person with certain beliefs and values. We have resistance to people or places that create adversity and opposition along our path. Our adventures through life and love show us our fears, our thinking patterns, and a unique way of life. We are introduced to mentors that teach us life can be different than what our fears or old patterns have us believe. As we begin to understand a new way of life, we begin a cycle of change. The outdated version of who we died off and an updated version of peace and understanding arises like a "phoenix from the ashes." We are stronger than before. We learn to love deeper from a place that is pure joy and happiness. We have let go of our old thoughts, patterns, and behaviors to live a life of serenity and peace.

We all have a story we have let define us to this point in our lives. It has given us strategies for survival and coping. We have all been through suffering, pain, heartbreak, and loss at some point. We have been both the victim and the heroes in our story or others. As we heal, we discover we no longer must identify with our past labels, identity, or the story that tries to pull us back. The truth is you get to course correct your life at any moment, rewrite a new ending, change your beliefs, and give a new meaning to your life. Time to divorce your old story and marry a new truth.

You are the hero of your own story. Your soul's journey is about finding your way from unbecoming everything you had to be for survival to who you can truly become for the last part of your journey.

A love letter to myself

DEAR SELF

I saw you struggle through your life, making challenging decisions. I understand you did the best you could in the past with
parenting and relationships. You were not the only one in those situations to parent and lead the way. You tried to see the best in others
and give them the benefit of the doubt. To be as present as you could
be. The unconsciousness of your daily life took over every day. It
was all you could do to just survive and get you through each day.
Please do not feel guilt for the choices you made. Your objectives
were with pure intentions. You may have loved too much, but that is
not terrible. Love and kindness are the greatest gifts anyone can give
and receive. You hoped for the best of situations or people, but
everything was out of your control.

Forgive yourself for holding on when you need to let go. Forgive
yourself for allowing someone's energy to take over yours. Forgive
yourself for losing yourself while giving too much to others. Forgive
yourself for the investments in others or work. Forgive yourself for
not putting yourself first. You can do it now that you know better.
Time is only lost to experience and lessons you may have never

learned. Take the time to appreciate your life now and make each moment count.

All the lessons you had, have made you the person you are today. Although you feel regretful and resentful, it is time to let it go. Release the past and keep moving forward. You are on the right path now. Your truth will set you free when you learn to surrender to your past. You can now learn to move forward with ease. Let go of everything that was or how you wanted it to be. Life changes, and so do you. The journey is not everything we want but everything it is meant to be.

You are enough and you will always be. You are beautiful, caring, loving and pure. Keep being you, and the people that are meant to be in your life will always find their way to you.

Love
Your best self.

Love yourself worthy

LIFE IS TOO short to give your power to anyone else, to live in misery or live anything but happy! You will have moments of unhappiness, sadness, and experiences you do not like. They are all about building resilience and making you the strong person you are meant to be in life.

When I learned that I was enough on my own, I freed my soul from the manipulation of others and guilt. I let go of trying to fit in, belong to something, or be liked by everyone. Somehow, I hit this stage at 45. When I had enough of being everything and everyone to everybody, I realized I must rediscover who I am and what I enjoy in my life. I realized I had settled for crumbs of love and worthiness, and I was relying on others to fill me up and make me happy and worthy. I took my power back!

I want to teach people you are worthy at any age or stage of your life to love yourself unconditionally. Acceptance of yourself, just the way you are in your imperfections, is loving. It is up to you to improve yourself to your best version as you start to deal with your demons or trauma from the past. These are yours to deal with and not bring forward as baggage into your relationships or pass it on as generational trauma.

If you question the love from your partner, love yourself worthy enough to walk away from it before you wonder where the years went trying to fix someone else's issues. It is not your job. Love yourself worthy enough to follow your heart in a job, a passion, a hobby, or a goal. Love yourself worthy enough to have the hard conversations with the people you love. You are worthy of love, but you must give it yourself first. You need to accept yourself fully. You need to know what your self-care and self-love look like and feel like to you. You need to know how to make yourself happy before anyone else. You need to be willing to walk away from the people, places, and things that do not align with you and make you unhappy.

Your value comes from within. Your worth should never come at the cost of sacrificing your physical or emotional health. You should never sacrifice or feel unworthy by the people you are with; they are not your people. Do not give them the power over you to make you feel less than worthy. Not everyone is capable of love, and not everyone is willing to do the work to make themselves a better person by healing their past. You are only responsible for your life, your emotions, and your self-worth!

It is not selfish to put yourself first. It is self-care. Your personal need before others' wants. Your life decisions with consideration of what is good for everyone involved. Not harm others! Do not give up your life and happiness in fear of making others unhappy. Your happiness comes first.

When you learn to love yourself worthy of everything you deserve, your life is full of experiences and joy that will make the lessons all worthwhile. Love comes from within; without it, you will always be searching to fill the void of temporary happiness. Searching for the goal of *I will be happy when...* or *I will feel loved when...* is always only temporary. Self-love is endless, and you get to decide what it feels and looks like. You learn to fill up your own cup, and everything else is a bonus. Learn to enjoy your own company and be happy alone.

Worthiness is a power we choose to give others, but we should maintain that power within us. When we give the power away, we can become easily manipulated to think we are not good enough, and if we are not good enough, how can we be loved enough. It is a cycle of vulnerability, and yet it takes courage to break the cycle. Taking back your power and knowing your worthiness is a choice of loving and accepting yourself unconditionally.

Love yourself without ego, feel the passion in your heart to be alive and walk through life confidently. Live each day with gratitude.

When you finally know your worth, you will be clear on your values and follow through with integrity. Every day that you are unclear in your values, you give others the opportunity to decide your worthiness. Without boundaries, you allow others to determine the value of your friendship or your relationship in which you allow them to show up. Every day you allow others not to overstep your boundaries. You teach them your standards, values, and tolerance of respect.

Knowing your worth allows you to set proper boundaries within your life and relationships with ease and less guilt. When you start learning to communicate and set boundaries, it is challenging to speak your truth.

- *Boundaries are about using your voice to ask for what you need or creating value for yourself.*
- *Boundaries allow you to take back your time, value, and power.*
- *Boundaries are for you, a way to reclaim your values and your needs.*
- *Boundaries will provide consequences on the actions you are willing to take if someone crosses the line.*

- *Boundaries are for your own self-care, self-discipline, and self-respect. You set your standards with accountability and integrity.*
- *Boundaries take work and need to be an ongoing process of learning, re-evaluating, and repeating.*
- *Boundaries are about learning to use both YES and No, when necessary, without guilt or blame for yourself or anyone else.*

KNOW YOUR WORTH!

Lessons come from Experience

Everyone has different beliefs, values, goals, priorities, and fears. We each need to find our own destination in life. Parents, teachers, and peers help guide us based on their knowledge and experience. Children teach us patience, perspective, and unconditional love. I am not sure we ever master anything in life. We just continue to learn from all the people around us if we are open to education. We never genuinely appreciate and value a parent until we become one and truly see the world through their experience. Then we call and apologize for what we did and didn't realize the outcomes. We take ownership because karma is showing us reality. Although we struggle to raise our own children, everyone has an opinion on how to raise everyone else's. Somehow, we think it would be easier, but we have no consequences if we are wrong.

Being vulnerable enough to admit blame and shame puts everything into perspective. Sometimes we want to blame others for our mistakes, and then we become ashamed of the situations we know we should have learned from. The first mistake is a lesson, the second time it is a choice.

"Lessons in Life will be repeated until learned." We will not like

every lesson or understand it. I finally understood that quote when I realized these were my lessons and no one else's. Sometimes I still need to remind myself of this when I become frustrated and overwhelmed with situations.

How do we learn from those experiences? The only way you truly learn anything is by doing it. We may screw up, but we learn from natural consequences. Everyone has their own agenda in their discovery path. We feel frustrated trying to teach others when really, the lesson is ours to learn. Allow them their own experiences and time frame. It is not up to us to save or fix others. Think about how hard it is to change your patterns and habits, so you can't be responsible for changing others, especially when they do not see an issue. They are not ready, and nothing you can do or say will make that happen. Change is only up to the individual when they are ready. When you focus on other people, you take away from your own healing journey. They may not be able to relate to the same information you do but plant the seeds and allow it to grow in time.

Learning who you truly are is a process; for some people, it takes longer to realize who they are and the right direction in life for them. Sometimes we struggle to be on the best path for us. Sometimes life gives us a detour so we can better understand the direction we need to go for a better life. If we always chose the right path, we would lack experiences of right and wrong. Most times in life, the best lessons are those we learn the hard way or on the wrong paths. So, if your path is not going to help you improve yourself and reach your goals, you may want to re-evaluate your priorities, the people you are with, and the direction you need to go to accomplish your dreams. You will realize your strengths in the moments you feel weakness. Some people are not this fortunate.... they give into weakness constantly. Weakness can come in many forms, other people and their issues, addictions, love, and abuse. Strength comes from knowing and believing you are important. This journey is all about you.

We never stop growing, learning, or living. Look at the world around you and where you fit into it. Are you living your life as you were meant to? Or are you fitting into someone else's life and someone else's dreams? What makes you happy? What are your greatest challenge, worst addiction, and biggest fear? Just when you think you have all the answers, life throws you a curveball to see how much more you can handle. This is a test of what you honestly believe in. Be up for any challenge, as the challenge is growth.

MY LESSONS

If you want to teach your children to understand the world, you cannot save them from the lessons the world (people) gives them.

We cannot expect a change in others if we are unwilling to change ourselves. Change starts with YOU.

Contradictions are all about changing our perspectives. "Change the way you look at things and the things you look at change," Dr. Wayne Dyer

Not everyone will conform to your expectations of life but remember it is your expectations of how life or people treat you. Not their expectations.

Love for the moment because the moment is the only thing in life guaranteed.

What makes you happy is not going to make everyone else happy. Everyone has a unique perspective on life, especially their own.

You can love people unconditionally and accept them whole-heartedly. This does not mean you share the same views, boundaries, and ethics.

When a situation does not fit with your life anymore, it is okay to walk away. It is always a choice only to be made by you.

The only way to genuinely love someone else is by learning to love yourself first. Enjoy your own company. At the end of the day, you are truly the only one that must live with YOU. So, if you do not like yourself, what makes you think anyone else will?

Sometimes my perspective of life is harder to live by because I am challenged daily by external forces that I need to consider and adapt. It is not just me I have to take into perspective, but those I love and live with.

Living with others takes a great deal of perspective, adaptability, accountability, responsibility, respect, and unconditional LOVE.

Not all situations are conducive to the way we believe life should be.

An ultimatum is giving the other person the final right to choose a path they feel is right for them, separate from their own boundaries, values, and ethics. Be strong enough to take control of making a decision that aligns with your life.

In creating boundaries and limitations within our life we choose how we live and our standards on how we want to be treated and live our life.

Love is knowing and accepting yourself and your boundaries, plus accepting someone else's boundaries and compromising on living a life of understanding and gratitude.

The past is our best teacher; you learn experiences from mistakes and realize the direction of the future path.

Loving unconditionally means I do not have to be in a relationship. I can still love them and walk away as I still have the choice.

I am in charge of my life. I can change, alter, and rediscover who I am whenever I choose. I am not confined to anyone.

My children have taught me the greatest lessons of my life!

My values and my beliefs are the only ones that dominate my life!

Show up, be seen just as you are, and the right people will love you as you are.

Listen when no words are spoken, for you will hear more in silence than you will with words.

Love when no one else will. Someday, you will need love and kindness in return.

Kindness takes no effort but lasts a long time for both the giver and receiver.

When someone is in depression, be the person that shows up for them and holds space exactly where they are.

Be BRAVE – make Boundaries, Be Respectful, Be Authentic, learn your Values and know the difference between Enabling and Empowering.

Love someone MORE than any argument you will have, more than any past situation and anything that will come between you.

Learn to BREATHE; your breath is just as valuable as time, the moment, or people. Once it is gone, there is nothing you can do to get it back.

People will condemn you for things they do not know, but truths are deeper than assumptions.

People will blame you when they are stuck in their ego and refuse to see there is a better way.

You may judge people on their past situations but be willing to see a different side when it is shown.

The lesson I learned from relationships was that when people seek the attention and love of others so much, they conform to the needs of others rather than understanding their authentic selves.

Do not feel guilty for choosing a life that is best for you, and never stay anywhere that makes you unhappy long term.

You only live once

You HAVE one life to live, and whether you make good choices or bad decisions, you need to find a way to heal from the past if it keeps you stuck. Heal from your own trauma, deal with your own recovery, forgive when possible and let go of the things you cannot control. You may not be responsible for the pain others caused you, but you are responsible for how you have let it affect your life. Don't let generational trauma win. Only you can change your present and your future.

Everything that has happened in your life has led you to this moment and who you are now. I know I would have made different decisions in life if I knew the outcome. But then, I may have never had my two beautiful children. All the great experiences of life, the most difficult challenges are the lessons I have overcome. All the relationships and friendships have taught me about who I am, what I like, and what my strengths are as a parent, a partner, and a friend. I do not regret that life happened the way it did, but I regret my choices in those moments. Life could have been different, but it wasn't, so I do not dwell on the "what ifs" or "what could have been." Those thoughts keep people stuck in the past. I do not regret the relationships because they taught me many lessons and showed me strength, compassion, and understanding for myself and future relationships.

Life has taught me to be strong in my values, be generous and have boundaries. Two things can be right. You can love someone and still walk away because loving yourself is more important than the love you can give to anyone. I can love my kids and still allow them their own journey without the expectation of always being there for them. I hope someday I will be closer with them, the one they can confide in and have the closeness we once had. They know I am always there for them. I have learned not to accept crumbs and think my cup is full. I can fill my life with everything that makes me happy. I choose my company and enjoy my own time. I have learned acceptance and love for myself that I do not need to change me or have anyone's point of validation that I am enough or loved enough. At the same time, I am blessed to have someone who believes in me and loves me more than anyone ever has. He makes my heart complete.

My children may not understand why I had to stay in an unhealthy relationship, and they have their own emotional baggage from it. Ultimately, it gave them strengths differently than if they lived a completely happy, unchaotic life. They learned their values, boundaries, and their own self-worth. They learned to trust their own instincts and go after what they wanted. Life is not always fair, and you must work for everything you have. They learned independence and gratitude. Hopefully, someday they will realize even in the times they did not think I took their side, I always did! I tried to stay neutral to avoid confrontation in front of them. When it came down to it, I always had their back; they just did not see it sometimes.

There are so many situations and experiences in our life that shape us into being bitter or better. Karma has a way of taking care of the people that wronged us, so we can choose to forgive them and ourselves for all our wrong decisions. Throughout our life we have different priorities that affect our decisions and the direction of our life. We make choices that meet our needs until we learn to meet our own needs with healthy distinction versus unhealthy preferences. Everyone has trauma in their life. It comes down to how you allow it to affect your life and emotions. You can play the victim, the hero, the warrior, and /or the survivor. You can hold on to it, feel helpless, or regain your power, forgive, and let go. You will always have challenges to overcome in your life. Build your resilience and help others when necessary. Give beyond yourself, always live in a state of gratitude, and take nothing for granted.

I hope you learn that you are worthy without validation, that you need to love and accept yourself without judgement and conditions. To genuinely love others unconditionally starts with how you treat yourself. Self-care is not selfish. It is necessary! You will not have the same values or boundaries as the next person. Do not lose yourself while trying to love someone and make them happy. You are enough alone, and any friendship or relationship is just a bonus.

Love yourself worthy of everything you deserve in your life. Not everyone wants or desires the same job, the same lifestyle, the same relationship, or the same riches. True love is special and rare. When you find it, invest in yourself and each other Love generously but remember love is not always enough if you are not happy. When you love and accept yourself unconditionally, you can receive the same love and give equal love to others.

Fall in love with yourself

Falling in love with yourself is the best gift you can give yourself and others. It does not happen overnight and takes years of growth. Shadow work and many conversations with yourself and sometimes talking with a therapist to pull out the weeds and discover the flowers. We all have demons and skeletons to hide from in our past and things we do not want to show or share with others. We fake a smile to fit in or try to belong. We pretend everything is good while dying inside. We pretend we are happy despite the survival mode and triggers we face every day. We fear others will dislike us if they know who we truly are. We sabotage our joy in fear by convincing ourselves we are not good enough. When you learn to fall in love with yourself, you will trade ego for confidence, your insecurities for values and boundaries. You will understand that everything in life is for a reason and loving others stems from how you love yourself. You let go of your inner critic or learn not to listen with harsh judgements. You create more acceptance for yourself and others around you, knowing that everyone is doing the best they can at the moment or is all they know or have been taught. Not everyone is open and willing to change; you are only responsible for your growth and life.

. . .

FALLING *in love with Myself*

Courage to walk away from the people and places that tore me down rather than help build me up.

Strength to overlook and let go of others' opinions of me and my life.

Vulnerability to be authentic and allow others to see me as I am.

Knowledge of what my triggers were so I could let go of the baggage and live my life happy.

Acceptance of loving me exactly as I am.

Boundaries, so I could be strong in my values and stand up for what I believe.

Forgiveness from all my past mistakes as they were lessons to build on for my future.

MOST OF ALL I learned that although I am not perfect, I am perfect for me and that loving unconditionally must start with loving and accepting myself unconditionally.

9 789655 780314